考研英语
阅读提分训练100篇
（基础版）

新东方考试研究中心 编著

试题册

群言出版社
QUNYAN PRESS

· 北 京 ·

重难点词汇音频

目 录

Text 1

In the silent ticket office, beneath the half-moon windows of the booths, a large green sign announces "OKEHAMPTON" to an empty room. On the platform, a faded poster reads "DEVON—Travel by rail". Those reading it have had little chance to do so. The last passenger train left Okehampton on June 3rd 1972. The town turned out to mourn: the mayor stood by, holding a wreath. On the line, between the sleepers, the grass started to grow.

But Okehampton is changing. New steel tracks gleam beneath the platform; diggers toil in the car park. The station is being reopened as part of the government's "Restoring Your Railway" fund, launched in January last year to keep a manifesto promise. Okehampton is the first to reopen. Eleven miles of track have been laid in four weeks.

In 1963 a report by Richard Beeching, chairman of the British Railways Board, earmarked 5,000 miles of track and 2,363 stations for closure. To this day, it is seen less as a piece of bureaucracy than as an act of "infamy"; it cuts "a wound that hasn't healed", according to Stewart Francis, a former chairman of the Rail Passengers' Council. On the Beeching "wound", Okehampton's 11 miles of shiny new track are a mere sticking plaster.

But to see this in terms of pure numbers is to miss the point. More than sleepers and steel were lost. "Railways have a strange position in the British mind," says John Preston, a professor of rail transport at the University of Southampton. "A lot of rural lines disappeared that were representative of a way of life...for which there was a lot of nostalgia," he notes. The new line is less about travelling through Devon than about travelling through time.

While lots of infrastructure is prosaic, in Britain trains become poetry, their lines not just crossing the land, but running on into the literature of Robert Louis Stevenson, John Betjeman and W. H. Auden. Restoring railways nods to this fictional Britain, a place of branch lines and straight backs, railway porters and station masters.

But poetry, while nice, has never been particularly profitable. There could hardly be a worse time for them to open: in the first COVID-19 lockdown passenger numbers fell by around 90％ and "the post-COVID demand path is not yet clear", says Mr. Preston. Still, in Okehampton the locals seem pleased. Becky Tipper, the Network Rail manager in charge of the reopening, was surprised when, as her workers started laying the track, "a crowd of people" turned out once again. This time, no wreaths. Instead, says Ms. Tipper, they started clapping.

1. According to the first two paragraphs, Okehampton _____.

    A) has changed a lot because of the train shutdown

    B) is the first beneficiary of a reconstruction plan

C) reopened its railway station last January

D) will become a symbol of British nostalgia

2. Richard Beeching was criticized for _____.

   A) his unrealistic report　　　　　　　　B) his bad temper

   C) damaging the British railway system　　D) causing irreparable emotional damage

3. The word "prosaic" (Line 1, Para. 5) is closest in meaning to _____.

   A) complex　　　　B) advanced　　　　C) broken　　　　D) ordinary

4. It is indicated in the last paragraph that _____.

   A) social benefit of railway restoration is greater than economic benefit

   B) only the locals along the rails can understand the value of the trains

   C) railway services should be reopened at a more appropriate time

   D) rail reconstruction may encounter some unexpected difficulties

5. What is the text centered on?

   A) The result of a survey.　　　　　　B) The effects of a lifestyle.

   C) The debates over a policy.　　　　　D) The background of a project.

Text 2

Ivorians celebrated when Eni, the Italian energy group, revealed that it had discovered up to 2bn barrels of oil in waters off the west African country—the first big find in two decades. Oil could start flowing within four years, boosting exports from a country that is already the world's biggest grower of cocoa.

But not everyone shares the confidence. While Ivory Coast is already pumping small quantities of oil, the risk was that it would bring more "on stream at a time when the market is already in decline", said Kingsmill Bond, an energy strategist. As advanced economies switch to electric vehicles and renewable energy, demand for oil will fall and only the lowest-cost producers will survive. Production costs of offshore African oil, especially in deep water, were relatively high, Bond added. Ivory Coast's find is at about 1,200 metres. Despite the surge in oil and gas prices this autumn, many analysts predict declining demand will force prices down, making higher-cost oil uncompetitive.

The find also taps into a broader debate about what it is reasonable to expect of developing countries that are reliant on fossil fuels. As the COP26 UN climate change summit in Glasgow approaches and many rich countries accelerate a shift towards clean energy, some governments in Africa are calling for a "just energy transition" that allows for a slower switch to other fuels. Governments in Africa, which are responsible for at most 3 per cent of global emissions, object to being pressed by banks and donors to abandon the fossil fuels on which they say their development depends.

Thomas Camara, energy minister, said that by 2030 the Ivorian government intended to increase the mix of renewable energy, currently entirely hydro, from 40 to 42 per cent of a much larger energy pie. "But we envisage our energy needs will go up significantly and we will need gas."

There was a danger the world was moving towards green energy without taking into account the huge needs of industrialisation in Africa and other poorer regions, said Kenny Fihla, chief executive of wholesale clients at Standard Bank, Africa's biggest lender. "It is nearly impossible to talk about Africa without oil at this stage," he said. "Even in 2050, there will still be some oil-utilisation, as other types of fuel will not have developed adequately to be able to replace it." Bond urged African governments to look with more urgency at developing solar and wind power which, he said, would prove to be both more abundant and cheaper than fossil fuels.

1. It is suggested that in Ivory Coast _____.
   A) overseas companies can exploit oil   B) cocoa may be the only product for export
   C) no energy source was found before   D) oil has been produced for four years
2. Bond considered oil exploitation risky because _____.
   A) competition in the oil industry got fiercer   B) the cost of oil production in Africa was low
   C) oil production was extremely difficult   D) renewable energy helped reduce oil demand
3. According to some governments in Africa, what is a "just energy transition"?
   A) Postponing the use of clean energy.   B) Obtaining investment and donations.
   C) Considering the oil needs of Africa.   D) Speeding the development of other fuels.
4. We can learn from Paragraphs 4 and 5 that African countries are _____.
   A) developing hydropower only
   B) experiencing industrialisation
   C) reluctant to bear the risk of energy transition
   D) unable to afford the utilisation of clean energy
5. Bond's attitude towards clean energy seemed to be _____.
   A) indifferent   B) unrealistic   C) optimistic   D) pessimistic

Text 3

Climate change is affecting us in ways no one could have imaged just a few years ago, and those dramatic changes in weather patterns may even affect your retirement. In recent years the world has been plagued by higher temperatures and increases in both the volume and intensity of natural disasters. You may need to incorporate the impact of climate change into your retirement planning.

Most people retire in place, meaning that they stay in the home they have lived in and raised a family. Those who relocate for retirement often choose warmer climates like Florida, Texas and Arizona. But before you relocate to a dream retirement spot with warmer weather, do your research. The increased incidence of wildfires, floods and hurricanes in states like Florida, Texas and California might give you reason to reconsider your relocation plans.

Climate change may impact your retirement budget, especially if you have to pay for air conditioning or to repair your home after a natural disaster. It may also be increasingly difficult or expensive to buy insurance for natural disasters. Dan Hawley, president of Hawley Advisors Wealth Planning, says his clients built a home at the foothills of the Sierra Nevada mountains and were shocked to find that their homeowner's insurance quadrupled to $4,000 a year.

Existing health problems could be exacerbated by environmental concerns such as extreme heat or wildfire smoke, with older adults more vulnerable to some of the health impacts of climate change. Those with limited mobility are often the most impacted by extreme weather events. What we call the urban heat island effect happens in areas like Washington, D.C., and New York, where there is a lot of concrete. That impacts health—diabetes, high blood pressure and asthma. And if you don't have cooling in your apartment or home, you're more likely to suffer one of those heat related events.

You may be able to make home improvements that could help the environment and perhaps even save your money over time. But consider making expensive changes while you still have steady income, before you retire. Many states and cities have programs that will subsidize solar panels. Consider replacing old appliances with more energy efficient models. New windows can be expensive, but they can dramatically increase energy efficiency.

Climate change offers opportunities for older Americans to get involved and volunteer. Older adults in retirement have time, experience and a motivation. One of the challenges of retirement for them is a sense of purpose. And for many of them older adults, climate action, and leaving the world a better place for their kids and grandkids for future generations, is an answer.

1. The author advises those who plan to relocate for retirement to _____.
   A) consider the impact of natural disasters　　B) stay in their original residence
   C) choose some warmer regions　　D) investigate the state governments fully

2. The example of Mr. Hawley's clients is mentioned to illustrate _____.
   A) the trouble of repairing your home
   B) the difficulty in purchasing a new house
   C) the deception of natural disaster insurance
   D) the possibility of increasing retirement budget

3. What should people do to deal with health risks brought by climate change?
   A) Move away from areas with urban heat island effect.
   B) Limit daily expenses as many as possible.
   C) Continue to use old and cheap appliances.
   D) Make costly changes before retirement.

4. One benefit of climate action involvement is that it enables the elderly in America to _____.
   A) forget bad social experiences　　B) have a sense of purpose
   C) overcome fears for the future　　D) maintain enthusiasm

5. This text is mainly about _____.
   A) ways to better arrange life in old age
   B) precautions against poor retirement planning
   C) the impact of climate change on retirement planning
   D) the risk of relocation brought by environmental issues

Text 4

Traffic congestion is a problem for cities around the world. One company believes the solution is to build a network of driverless high-speed pods that ride around cities suspended from a steel track.

In June, Belarus-based uSky Transport opened a 400-meter test line in Sharjah, which borders Dubai in the United Arab Emirates (UAE). A fully implemented city-wide network could support 10,000 passengers per hour, uSky says, with vehicles currently able to travel up to 150 kilometers per hour —although for safety reasons, they can't reach their top speed on the test track. According to uSky, while one kilometer of subway can cost up to $150 million to construct, this system costs around $10 million. And by using less structural materials, it reduces carbon emissions.

Though "sky pods" are often compared to monorails or cable cars, they offer greater flexibility, says Stephanie Haag, associate partner at consulting firm McKinsey & Company. "In a cable car, you have one car and it always drives at the same speed," she says. "In sky pods you can use many different cabins on that particular infrastructure," such as ones tailored for shorter trips in urban areas or for longer distances. Although she cautions that it would require careful planning to avoid congestion in a busy city-wide network, Haag believes it could still be a widely adopted solution if the promises of improved mobility and sustainability are kept.

Later this year, uSky plans to build a 2.4 kilometer line in Sharjah, allowing it to run the passenger pod at higher speeds and demonstrate how passenger and cargo pods can be integrated into the same network. With the test line up and running, uSky has also received initial approval to build a line around the coastal town of Khor Fakkan, to the east of the emirate.

Neighboring emirate Dubai is also exploring driverless pods that would operate above city traffic and other global companies are reportedly developing high-tech transport pods for the region.

Oleg Zaretskiy, uSky Transport's CEO, says uSky is also looking beyond the UAE. "We can see that the most promising areas for us are in the Middle East and Asia—places where there is natural growth of population, such as India and Pakistan," he says.

Haag adds that pods are more suited to countries where public transportation is underdeveloped and there is increasing demand for mobility solutions. Still, Zaretskiy says uSky Transport has received inquiries from countries including the United States and Canada. The company hopes to finalize its first commercial contract by the end of the year in Sharjah, Zaretskiy adds, meaning uSky pods could be up and running over traffic by 2024.

1. It can be learned from the first two paragraphs that uSky Transport _____.
   A) hopes to ease traffic congestion in an artificial intelligent way
   B) attempts to set up a network of driverless high-speed pods
   C) has reduced the construction cost of rail transportation
   D) focuses on the development of low-carbon transportation
2. According to Stephanie Haag, the "sky pods" _____.
   A) will solve the problem of traffic congestion B) are more suitable for long-distance travel
   C) provide passengers with greater flexibility D) always travel at a constant speed

3. The development of the driverless system of "sky pods" _____.

    A) attracts the attention of many countries   B) achieves its first breakthrough in Dubai

    C) is mainly undertaken by uSky Transport   D) receives a warm welcome from customers

4. According to Mr. Zaretskiy, this new way of transportation _____.

    A) may first benefit the underpopulated Middle East

    B) is expected to come into service in the near future

    C) hasn't encountered a mature market opportunity

    D) will play a better role in the less developed areas

5. In this text, the author mainly attempts to _____.

    A) recommend a few companies that develop new vehicles

    B) put forward some suggestions to ease urban traffic jams

    C) discuss possible development of some traffic modes in the future

    D) introduce futuristic pods designed to solve traffic problems

(Text 5)

A year ago, my 58-year-old otherwise healthy father contracted COVID-19. He eventually succumbed to it, and died. And I have been dealing with the grief ever since, while under lockdown. If you go by how it is portrayed in mainstream fiction, grief is very predictable. You go through five stages: denial, anger, bargaining, depression and acceptance. Once through all these stages, you can move on with your life. But reality is far more complex. Elisabeth Kübler-Ross, who came up with the five-stage idea, regretted writing it in such a way that led to its simplistic portrayal.

Grief during lockdown is even more complex. I say this as someone who, like millions of other people, has endured months of it, cut off from friends and family. I fear this is causing genuine problems that are going unrecognised or unacknowledged. Our brains learn and develop based on our experiences and understanding of the world around us. So, even if inaccurate or oversimplified, the cultural consensus about grief informs our expectations. We "know" that when you lose someone, you have a funeral and wake to say goodbye to or celebrate the departed. These accepted parts of the grieving process are thrown out of whack by lockdown.

And while well intentioned, socially distanced funerals may do more harm than good. Among other things, rituals give the bereaved a sense of control over events, something important for well-being. To have it limited to 14 next of kin? Nobody wanted that. What are the consequences for well-being if a funeral makes you feel less in control, rather than more?

Delayed grief, where the effects hit later, or complex grief, where someone has disruptive reactions to a loss beyond what is deemed normal, are conditions recognised by medical science. It could be that these problems arise because the experience of grief doesn't match the expectations our brains have formulated. Maybe I will experience the full effects of grief long after my father's passing, when lockdown in the UK finally fully ends and my father not being there becomes "real". This might make me and everyone else in the same situation mentally unwell.

As understandable as it is, from my perspective as both a grieving relative and a neuroscientist, the current "Hooray, no more lockdown!" attitude of much of the UK media and general public only throws the enduring grief of many into stark relief. While it is fine to embrace the improving situation regarding the pandemic in the UK, we should be in no rush to "move on" and pretend it never happened, or to condemn or sideline those still feeling the effects of what it took from them. That could make a bad situation worse.

1. The five-stage theory of grief _____.

A) can help people cope with grief in a predictable way

B) offers a simplified view of how people deal with grief

C) describes a much longer period of anger

D) covers all responses people can have in great sadness

2. It is indicated in Paragraph 2 that a funeral _____.

A) represents the end of our grieving procedure B) is an inappropriate occasion for celebration

C) is an expected part when we lose someone   D) has unrecognised benefits to the bereaved

3. The author mentions the limited number of kin at the funeral to illustrate _____.

A) the rigid regulations on rituals   B) the vogue for socially distanced funerals

C) the popularity of his beloved father   D) the feeling of less control

4. One possible result of delayed grief is _____.

A) a changed expectation   B) the denial of reality

C) a mental problem   D) an abnormal relationship

5. What does the author argue in the last paragraph?

A) People who are suffering delayed grief need others' empathy.

B) The media should stop the celebration of the end of lockdown.

C) It is wrong for the grieving few to exaggerate their depression.

D) The enduring grief would come to a natural end after lockdown.

(Text 6)

Platform shoes are back in fashion, at least in athletics. Many of the long-distance runners at the Tokyo Olympics, which begin on July 23rd, will arrive at the starting line sporting footwear with a distinctive chunky-looking heel. It will be more than just a fashion statement. The new shoes offer such a big performance advantage that critics have described them as "technological doping".

Running-shoe makers have long tried to boost athletic performance, observes Geoff Burns, a biomechanics expert at the University of Michigan. In olden days, a 1% improvement in "running economy"—the energy taken to travel a given distance—would have impressed. But in 2016 Nike released the first version of its "Vaporfly" model, which improved running economy by 4%.

If that percentage were to translate directly into performance, it would knock about five minutes off an elite male's marathon time. In practice, as Dr. Burns observes, it wouldn't quite do that. A marathon improvement of around 90 seconds would be a more realistic expectation. But Vaporfly and its successors have helped athletes smash a string of records. On June 6th, Sifan Hassan, a

Dutch runner, completed a women's 10,000 metres race in 29 minutes and 6.82 seconds, beating a record set in 2016.

Scientists are still puzzling over exactly how the shoes work. The soles are made of a new type of foam that offers the unprecedented resilience, according to Dr. Burns. This returns around 80% of the energy from each strike of a runner's foot. The carbon-fibre plate may help by stiffening the midsole, and possibly by altering a runner's way of walking. By cushioning a runner's bones and muscles from repetitive impacts, the shoes may even help athletes train harder than they otherwise could.

All that is great news for Nike, which sells the Vaporfly and its successors for around $250 each. Whether it is good for the sport is another question. Different sports have different tolerances for technological assistance. Running tends towards the conservative end of the spectrum.

In January 2020, World Athletics, the governing body of international athletics, passed new rules limiting the thickness of a road shoe's sole to 40mm. Meanwhile, Nike appears to have shelved plans to deploy high tech shoes designed for sprinters at the Tokyo games, possibly because they did not comply with regulations either. But if they, or a rival manufacturer, have worked out a way around that problem, there could be fireworks in the sprints, too.

1. Why does the author say using platform shoes is "more than just a fashion statement"?
    A) Because the shoes are out of fashion now.   B) Because the shoes look remarkably chunky.
    C) Because the shoes improve running economy. D) Because the shoes can take the place of dope.
2. Which of the following statements about "running economy" is right?
    A) It measures how labor-saving the running is.
    B) It shows the progress of making sports shoes.
    C) It may improve the performance of runners.
    D) It is a concept about long-distance running.
3. The case about long-distance running in Paragraph 3 is mentioned to _____.
    A) refute the arguments of Dr. Burns   B) praise the breakthroughs in running
    C) explain how the platform shoes work   D) show the influence of platform shoes
4. Except for improving athletic performance, platform shoes can also _____.
    A) massage the runners' bones and muscles   B) correct the athletes' inappropriate behaviors
    C) provide runners with unprecedented comfort D) enable athletes to endure more tough training
5. The author holds that the prospect of platform shoes is _____.
    A) gloomy   B) hopeful   C) exciting   D) ambiguous

(Text 7)

In the past two or three years artificial intelligence has felt like rocket science. We have been wowed by developments in areas such as computer vision, machine translation and speech recognition. In 2020, AI will begin to live up to the hype by starting to generate real economic value through its application across industries. According to consulting firm PricewaterhouseCoopers, the widespread adoption of AI will add about $15.7 trillion to global GDP by 2030. Most of that business value will come not from AI-focused companies, but from the infusion of artificial intelligence into traditional industries. Early movers who embrace AI will become the winners.

One defining area of AI infusion is in the automation of repetitive tasks, using technologies such as RPA (robotic process automation). Routine tasks associated with a large number of jobs will now lend themselves to automation, freeing up people's time to focus on more complex endeavours. Another similar area of routine task replacement is the use of speech recognition and natural-language processing in customer service, telemarketing and telesales. New advances in these technologies allow 80 per cent of queries to a call centre to be dealt with through automated processes, while achieving higher customer satisfaction.

In addition to optimising existing processes, in future we will see new applications for AI across existing industries. Retail stores will use AI to forecast demand and sales, as well as to reshape logistics and the supply chain. AI will also help maximise production output and minimise costs in manufacturing and agriculture.

Healthcare will start to be significantly transformed by AI. While it will take several decades for AI to be fully integrated into the medical process, it is in 2020 that we will start to fully grasp AI's potential for improving our quality of life. Expect strides to be made in the application of smart AI tools in radiology, pathology and diagnosis—leading to better treatment, faster recuperation, and lower cost. Unlike RPA and speech recognition, these tools will not replace humans, but will help them be more productive.

AI will bring personalisation to many other areas too, including banking, insurance, loans and investment. We have already seen personal recommendations of news, content and merchandise, and we will see this continue to expand.

And in education we will see AI being used to give and grade homework and exams, and to guide students through various exercises. This will free up teachers' time to focus on students' personal and emotional development, in areas such as resilience, empathy, creativity and compassion—qualities that will be critical to the new generations' ability to thrive and adapt in the age of AI. In 2020, we will see AI, though still incredibly complex, start to become part and parcel of problem-solving across our lives.

1. Artificial intelligence resembles rocket science in _____.
    A) its rapid development   B) its application in computer vision
    C) its economic value   D) its infusion into traditional industries
2. The word "embrace" (Line 7, Para. 1) can be replaced by _____.
    A) hug   B) include   C) adopt   D) squeeze
3. According to Paragraph 2, the application of artificial intelligence may result in _____.
    A) the disappearance of all repetitive tasks   B) people's focus on more complicated work
    C) the replacement of all human service   D) higher satisfaction with the new tech
4. In 2020, artificial intelligence may help people to _____.
    A) significantly decrease production output   B) completely change the medical process
    C) continuously improve personalized service   D) fully prepare teachers for the age of AI

5. The author's attitude toward artificial intelligence is one of _____ .
   A) passive acceptance   B) slight hesitancy
   C) severe criticism   D) full approval

Text 8

The United States is not expected to electrify passenger cars fast enough to stay on track with the Paris Agreement's goal of limiting global warming to 2°C, according to a new study. Published in the journal *Nature Climate Change* yesterday, the study by engineers at the University of Toronto concludes that 90% of light-duty cars on American roads would need to be electric by 2050 to keep the transportation sector in line with climate mitigation targets.

That might mean requiring all of the nation's new car sales to be electric as early as 2035. If the target were adopted and implemented nationally, 350 million electric cars would ply the roads in 2050. Those would fuel up using the equivalent of 41% of the nation's total power demand in 2018, creating challenges for the grid.

Instead of focusing exclusively on switching from gas cars to battery-electrics or fuel-cell vehicles, said lead author Alexandre Milovanoff, policymakers should simultaneously aim to reduce the public's dependence on personal cars.

Over coming decades, the number of miles covered by cars is projected to continue increasing. Even if travel demand were frozen at current levels, 51% of all cars on the road in the United States would need to be electrics in 2050 to meet emissions targets set out in the Paris Agreement. That would mean achieving 30% of new car sales by 2030, a goal laid out by the International Energy Agency three years ago.

Huge infusions of money for public transit would be necessary to significantly reduce the nation's reliance on passenger cars. "It has to be about equity," Milovanoff said of carbon dioxide reductions. "It's about making sure all communities can access these systems." Land use changes could make it easier for people to live closer to their destinations, as well as to get around on foot or bicycle. New road tolls or taxes on car sales could discourage drivers from buying or using their own cars.

The authors noted another option for driving down emissions: fuel efficiency rules based on a vehicle's weight rather than the "footprint" approach. That would encourage car companies to roll out smaller, less energy-intensive models. That change would better align U.S. and European standards. The grid's carbon intensity would also prove crucial in determining the effect of EV adoption. The authors assumed that the U.S. electric grid is decarbonized by 2050, combining the use of carbon capture technology, renewable energy and nuclear power.

"So many cities in the U.S. don't even have pavement for pedestrians, or a well-developed subway or bus system," Milovanoff said. "It comes from the fact that these cities are vehicle-centered. They're built on the premise that we'll always use vehicles."

1. What do we know about the Paris Agreement?

   A) It requires electrification of private cars.   B) It is working on limiting global warming.

   C) It focuses on the use of light-duty cars in U.S. D) It will cease to be effective by the year 2050.

2. What does the word "ply" (Line 2, Para. 2) most probably mean?

   A) Travel along.   B) Block in.   C) Rebuild.   D) Destroy.

3. Which of the following measures may encourage people to give up using private cars?

   A) To publicize green travel in urban areas.

   B) To rationalize the land use of the U.S. cities.

   C) To invest a huge sum of money in passenger cars.

   D) To set up more toll stations along the roads.

4. What Milovanoff said in the last paragraph reveals that _____.

   A) Americans don't like public transportation

   B) it takes time to build a public transport system

   C) urban planning in the United States is unreasonable

   D) it is not easy to reduce the use of vehicles

5. Which of the following would be the best title for the text?

   A) The Paris Agreement Set an Unrealistic Objective

   B) Probing the Ways to Reduce the Use of Private Cars

   C) To Meet Climate Goals: Still a Long Way to Cover

   D) Ninety Percent of U.S. Cars Will Be Electric by 2050

(Text 9)

Vegan food is a "rip off", with customers paying up to 180 per cent more than for equivalent meat-based products, according to research. An analysis of prices at seven supermarkets found that four in five vegan products were more expensive than their meat alternatives, while more than half came in smaller sizes. Taking into account the weight of the products, the vegan versions were 26 per cent more expensive on average, despite containing ingredients that are many times cheaper. The analysis suggests that families choosing vegan alternatives to meat could be paying hundreds of pounds more a year for their food.

The research comes at the end of this year's "Veganuary", which saw a record half a million people pledge to go plant-based for a month. Supermarkets have been investing huge amounts in marketing to encourage customers to buy vegan food, introducing ranges and giving significant aisle space to their products.

Last month Tesco and M&S both released their first "Veganuary" TV and radio adverts, while Waitrose, Aldi, Asda, Iceland and Morrisons launched dedicated "Veganuary" web pages. Tesco says that demand for vegan alternatives to meat was up by more than a third in January compared with the previous year. The researchers noted that the growing popularity of veganism was presenting the supermarkets with an opportunity for "serious profits". However, supermarkets argue that vegan foods often have higher production costs because of the complex processes used to create them.

The study found that M&S's Plant Kitchen "No Pork" sausage rolls cost £2.25 for a 120g serving but that the same weight of M&S pork sausage rolls cost only 80p, making the vegan choice nearly three times the price. The meat version's main ingredient is pork, followed by wheat flour, while the vegan version's main ingredient is wheat flour followed by palm oil, water, pea protein, onions and mushrooms. Pork is about eight times more expensive wholesale than wheat.

An estimated 600,000 British people are vegan and a further 1.2 million vegetarian but increasing numbers are adopting a "flexitarian" diet where they go some days without meat. Supporters of vegan foods say that they are healthier and better for the environment. However, meat farmers have disputed that and have showcased research that suggests that eating tofu is worse for the planet than consuming most lamb, pork or chicken.

Nutritionists have also raised concerns about veganism, warning that it may leave people short of essential micronutrients and at risk of poor bone health and other conditions. The Vegan Society has refuted these claims, saying that "well-planned" vegan diets contain all the nutrients our bodies need.

1. What does the phrase "rip off" (Line 1, Para. 1) most probably mean?
   A) To tear something or to become torn, often suddenly or violently.
   B) To steal something from somebody.
   C) To cheat somebody by charging too much money.
   D) To remove something quickly or violently.

2. The aisle space in the supermarket is mentioned to indicate _____.
   A) the importance supermarkets attached to vegan products
   B) the popularity of vegan products
   C) the wide variety of vegan products
   D) the large number of vegan products on sale

3. Supermarkets justify the high price of vegan food by saying that _____.
   A) they have to advertise on TV, radio or the website
   B) the demand for vegan products is too high to meet
   C) they face fierce competition in the market
   D) the production of the vegan food is at a high cost

4. In the dispute regarding veganism, there is scientific evidence that _____.
   A) vegan foods lead to healthier life and cleaner environment
   B) eating tofu is worse for the Earth than eating meat
   C) vegan foods lead to a lack of trace minerals
   D) tailored vegan diets make us healthier

5. The author's attitude toward veganism is _____.
   A) biased   B) objective   C) subjective   D) indifferent

(Text 10)

There has been a quiet pandemic developing while most people's attention has been on COVID-19. The lockdown has aggravated a problem that has been spreading in many developed nations for decades: loneliness.

Part of the problem stems from contemporary employment. Globally, two in five office workers feel lonely at work. This rises to three in five in Britain. Gig-economy jobs can leave people with insecure incomes and without the companionship of colleagues. The pandemic has made it more difficult to make, and maintain, friendships, particularly for new employees.

It may seem odd that loneliness can grow when people are surrounded by so many others. But this paradox was best expressed by the band Roxy Music, when they sang "Loneliness is a crowded room". Most people will be perfectly content, for a while at least, eating on their own at home, perhaps with a good book or a TV programme. Sitting all alone in a restaurant or a bar, surrounded by other people chatting, is a much more isolating affair.

By the same token, big cities can be very isolating. In a survey from 2016, 55% of Londoners and 52% of New Yorkers said they sometimes felt lonely. In many cities, around half of all residents live on their own, and the average tenancy of a London renter lasts 20 months. City-dwellers are less likely to be polite, because they are unlikely to meet a passer-by again. Perhaps this relates to human history. Mass urbanisation is a relatively recent development; if the history of human existence was squeezed into a single day, the Industrial Revolution did not occur until almost midnight. For much of that time, humans lived in small groups of hunter-gatherers; cities may just overwhelm the senses.

There are two more recent developments. The first is social media. The Internet has led to much cyber-bullying. And people glued to their smartphones spend less time interacting socially. The second is "neoliberalism". Some changes in behaviour are down to individual choice. Before the pandemic no one was stopping people going to church or taking part in sports. They simply preferred to do other things. Indeed, one reason for the decline in communal activities is that people choose to be with their families rather than head to the bar.

So recreating a communal society may be difficult. When the pandemic ends, people may relish the chance to be with their neighbours and colleagues for a while. But the trend is clear. Technology means that people can get their entertainment at home, and work there, too. It is convenient but it also leads to loneliness. Society will be grappling with this trade-off for decades to come.

1. What does "a quiet pandemic" (Line 1, Para.1) refer to?
   A) The spread of COVID-19.
   B) People's attention.
   C) The lockdown.
   D) Loneliness.
2. "Loneliness is a crowded room" is mentioned in Paragraph 3 to present _____.
   A) a supporting example
   B) an amusing episode
   C) a background story
   D) a related topic
3. Big-city dwellers feel lonely maybe because _____.
   A) they live alone and often move around
   B) they are too detached to greet each other
   C) they prefer the life in smaller habitations
   D) they are impacted by the mass urbanisation

4. The author suggests in Paragraph 5 that _____.

    A) genuine friendship can hardly be found on the Internet

    B) smartphones have reduced some face-to-face interaction

    C) the pandemic hasn't really influenced public activities

    D) more men prefer to stay at home with their families than women

5. What is the text centered on?

    A) Some suggestions on solving urban problems.

    B) Some negative effects of rapid urbanisation.

    C) The complex causes of widespread loneliness.

    D) A deep probe into mental state of city dwellers.

(Text 11)

As lawmakers and security researchers continue to unravel the SolarWinds hack, some are growing more frustrated with Amazon.com Inc., saying the cloud-computing giant should be more publicly forthcoming about its knowledge of the suspected cyberattack.

There are no indications that Amazon's systems were directly breached, but hackers used its sprawling cloud-computing data centers to launch a key part of the attack, according to security researchers. The operation has been described as one of the worst instances of cyber espionage in the nation's history.

While cybersecurity experts say it is nearly impossible to prevent hackers from misusing cloud services, as is alleged to have occurred in this case, they also say Amazon is likely sitting on critical information that could shed light on the scope of the attacks and the tactics used by the cybercriminals. Amazon has shared this information privately with the U.S. government, but unlike other technology companies, it is unwilling to making it public.

During a hearing of the Senate Intelligence Committee this week, senators—including Mark Warner, the Democratic chairman of the committee, and Marco Rubio, the Republican vice chairman—expressed irritation that Amazon declined to attend and said its insight into the hacking activity could prove valuable to lawmakers and the public. Some suggested obliquely that the panel should consider summoning testimony from the company.

"Amazon is not affected by the SolarWinds issue, and we do not use their software," an Amazon Web Services spokesman said. "When we learned of this event, we immediately investigated, ensured we weren't affected, and shared what we learned with law enforcement. We've also provided detailed briefings to government officials, including members of Congress."

Amazon's data centers housed servers that were used in a critical stage of the SolarWinds attack—the point when hackers had created a beachhead on their victims' networks and were looking for ways to probe systems for more information, security researchers said. Amazon's servers were used to host and deliver the hacking tools that were ultimately downloaded to victims' computers and then used to probe and break into new systems on these networks, they said. The cloud-computing company could have financial information on how its services were paid for, network traffic data showing whom the SolarWinds hackers interacted with on the internet, and data stored on the servers themselves showing what other activity the hackers were engaged in and possibly what other tools they were using.

Amazon, like all major technology companies, employs a "threat intelligence" team to track and protect customers and itself against known hacking groups. Because of their dominant market positions, these technology companies are increasingly informed of vast amounts of data that are often useful in investigating, detecting and removing malicious cyber adversaries.

1. According to the first two paragraphs, some people are urging Amazon to _____.
   A) inquire into the SolarWinds hack
   B) deepen its understanding of hackers
   C) share useful information with the public
   D) strengthen prevention against cyberattacks
2. Cybersecurity experts seem to believe that _____.
   A) hackers attacked a key part of Amazon's systems
   B) hackers used the information launched by Amazon
   C) some misuse of cloud service may not be prosecuted
   D) Amazon's data are helpful to investigate cyber crimes
3. Why did Amazon decline to attend the hearing of the Senate Intelligence Committee?
   A) Because it thought it had done all it could do.
   B) Because it refused to share information.
   C) Because it doubted the fairness of the hearing.
   D) Because it was tired of the SolarWinds investigation.
4. We can know from Paragraph 6 that _____.
   A) Amazon's data centers were often under attack
   B) Amazon's servers may be related to hacking
   C) Amazon probed into the computers of victims
   D) Amazon understood hackers' financial status
5. What is the author's attitude towards Amazon's statement?
   A) Supportive.   B) Favourable.   C) Indifferent.   D) Disapproving.

(Text 12)

Even before taking office, president-elect Joe Biden is already facing a political storm among his ideologically diverse base of supporters over the volatile issue of student-debt forgiveness.

Roughly 45 million Americans currently hold $1.6 trillion in student debt, with the average student-loan recipient owing between $20,000 and $25,000, according to the Federal Reserve. Among those actively making payments on their debt, the average monthly installment is between $200 and $300. And with 5.3 million more people unemployed than in February, right before the U.S. fell into a pandemic-induced recession, progressives say that student-debt forgiveness could be a boon for the economy.

"Student-debt cancellation feels like one of the most accessible executive actions to stimulate the economy at the moment," says Suzanne Kahn, director of the Education, Jobs and Worker Power program and the Great Democracy Initiative at the liberal Roosevelt Institute. Kahn and others say the move would also help close the wealth gap between white Americans and people of color. Some 90% of Black students and 72% of Latino students take out loans for college vs. just 66% of white students, according to a 2016 analysis from the Consumer Financial Protection Bureau.

But the more moderate faction of Biden's base argues that sweeping student-loan forgiveness doesn't help the people who need aid most. Americans with college degrees, as a whole, have been less devastated by the economic effects of COVID-19 than their noncollege-educated counterparts. A September report from Pew Research Center found that only 12% of people with college degrees were having trouble paying bills as a result of the pandemic, compared with 34% of Americans with a high school diploma or less.

Others raise concerns about precedent: if the government wipes out current student loans, future college students may have an incentive to take on debts, they argue, hoping they will also be forgiven. Colleges may in turn be inclined to raise their prices further.

In recent weeks, Biden has walked a fine line on the issue, offering support for a bill from House Democrats calling for $10,000 worth of student-loan forgiveness but stopping short of endorsing anything close to a plan championed by Senators Elizabeth Warren and Chuck Schumer to issue $50,000 per borrower through Executive action.

What's clear, according to experts on both sides of the aisle, is that economic crises aggravate the problem of student debt. The last time the U.S. dipped into a recession, state governments cut their investments in colleges and universities—which, in turn, raised their tuition prices and forced students to take on ever larger loans. That's not sustainable in the long run. It remains to be seen if Biden can arrive at a political solution that is.

1. The word "volatile" (Line 2, Para. 1) is closest in meaning to _____.
   A) disputed   B) embarrassing   C) ambiguous   D) neglected
2. The data cited in Paragraph 2 reveal _____.
   A) the debt crisis caused by unemployment   B) the situation of the American recession
   C) the great amount of student debt   D) the huge cost of higher education
3. According to Suzanne Kahn, student-debt forgiveness _____.
   A) contributes to economic development   B) can only be selectively implemented
   C) is most needed by people of color   D) may promote educational equality
4. Those who question student-debt forgiveness argue that _____.
   A) people with higher education are able to pay their debts
   B) difficulties caused by the pandemic are just temporary
   C) the government cannot afford more student loans
   D) debt forgiveness may lead to higher tuition fees

5. The author feels that the prospect of solving the student-debt problem is _____.

    A) pessimistic   B) promising   C) mysterious   D) uncertain

(Text 13)

Success in manufacturing depends on physical things: creating the best product using the best equipment with components assembled in the most efficient way. Success in the service economy is dependent on the human element: picking the right staff members and motivating them correctly. If manufacturing is akin to science, then services are more like the arts. Motivating people has an extra complexity. Widgets do not know when they are being manipulated. Workers make connections with their colleagues, for social or work reasons, which the management might not have anticipated.

Marissa King is professor of organizational behavior at the Yale School of Management, where she tries to make sense of these networks. The term "networking" has developed unfortunate connotations, suggesting the kind of person who sucks up to senior staff and ignores colleagues who are unlikely to help them win promotion. Ms. King cites a study which found that two-thirds of newly promoted professionals were ambivalent about, or completely resistant to, thinking strategically about their social relationships.

From the point of view of productivity, the most important networks are those formed by employees from different parts of the company. Diverse viewpoints should lead to greater creativity. They are good for workers, too. A study found that catching up with colleagues in different departments was linked to salary growth and employee satisfaction.

Some employers had the bright idea of encouraging this co-operation by moving to open-plan offices. But research suggests that workers in open-plan layouts are less productive, less creative and less motivated than those in offices with a traditional, room-based design. The quality of interactions is more important than the quantity. The pandemic, by forcing many people to toil away at home, has probably destroyed some of these co-operative arrangements.

Two fun case studies outline a common problem—the tendency for people to have too narrow a focus. In one test, only one in four mobile-phone users noticed a clown who unicycled past them while they were looking at their screens. In another revealing story, Catholic seminarians strode past a distressed bystander while in a hurry to give a lecture on the parable of the good Samaritan. In the right network, the presence of a diverse set of participants may allow the group to see the bigger picture.

Old-fashioned concepts like courtesy can also help, Ms. King argues. Simple gestures—a smile, a thank you—make colleagues more likeable and increase co-operation. In contrast, studies of workers who experience incivility find that their effort, time spent at work and commitment to the job all reduce. Ms. King invokes the aphorism that "assholes" can be identified by observing how they treat people with less power. "Don't be an asshole" is not a scientific statement. But it is still a pretty good management motto.

1. The author argues in the first paragraph that motivating employees correctly _____.
   A) depends on the best physical equipment   B) is key to the success in the service economy
   C) needs to use artistic techniques   D) goes beyond the management domain

2. The phrase "sucks up to" (Line 3, Para. 2) is closest in meaning to _____.
   A) flatters   B) detests   C) imitates   D) challenges

3. In terms of productivity, developing networks in the workplace _____.
   A) is irresistible for senior staff   B) causes conflicts among colleagues
   C) can be quite beneficial   D) leads to salary satisfaction

4. The two case studies in Paragraph 5 highlight the necessity to _____.
   A) focus on the surroundings   B) care for others' suffering
   C) build healthy networks   D) broaden our horizons

5. By saying "Don't be an asshole", Ms. King encourages people to _____.
   A) establish cooperation by being polite   B) become more engaged in their work
   C) identify the qualities of co-workers   D) treat the vulnerable people well

(Text 14)

A retired couple have become the world's first tenants of a fully 3D-printed house in a development that its backers believe will open up a world of choice in the shape and style of the homes of the future. Elize Lutz, 70, and Harrie Dekkers, 67, former shopkeepers from Amsterdam, received their digital key—an app allowing them to open the front door of their two-bedroom bungalow at the press of a button—yesterday. "It is beautiful," said Lutz. "It has the feel of a bunker—it feels safe," added Dekkers.

Inspired by the shape of a boulder, the dimensions of which would be difficult and expensive to construct using traditional methods, the property is the first of five homes planned by a construction firm for a plot of land by the Beatrix canal in the Eindhoven suburb.

In the past two years, properties partially constructed by 3D printing have been built in France and the US, and nascent projects are proliferating around the world. But those behind the Dutch house, which has 94 sq metres (1,000 sq ft) of living space, are said to have pipped their rivals to the post by making the first legally habitable and commercially rented property where the load-bearing walls have been made using a 3D printer nozzle. This is also the first one which is 100% permitted by the local authorities and which is inhabited by people who actually pay for living in this house," said Bas Huysmans, the chief executive of Weber Benelux.

The 3D printing method involves a huge robotic arm with a nozzle that squirts out a specially formulated cement, said to have the texture of whipped cream. The cement is "printed" according to an architect's design, adding layer upon layer to create a wall to increase its strength. The point at which the nozzle head had to be changed after hours of operation is visible in the pattern of the new bungalow's walls, as are small errors in the cement printing, perhaps familiar to anyone who has used an inkjet printer.

But while it is early days, the 3D printing method is seen by many in the construction industry as a way to cut costs and environmental damage by reducing the amount of cement used. In the Netherlands, it also provides an alternative at a time when there is a shortage of skilled bricklayers.

1. What can we know from the first paragraph about the retired couple?

    A) They support using the 3D printing method to build a bunker.

    B) They decided on the shape and style of the house that they would rent.

    C) They are quite content with the property that is leased to them.

    D) They had a very successful career when working in Amsterdam.

2. A boulder is mentioned in Paragraph 2 to illustrate that _____.

    A) building huge houses will face a lot of trouble

    B) traditional methods of construction are costly

    C) construction by the canal is extremely difficult

    D) the design of the property is inspired by the shape of it

3. What does the phrase "pip...to the post" (Lines 3~4, Para. 3) most probably mean?

    A) To transfer from one place to another.   B) To win in a competition or a race.

    C) To make an event known to all the people.   D) To ridicule others' ideas or beliefs.

4. It is indicated in Paragraph 4 that the nozzle _____.

    A) can only work for a short period   B) can produce spotless walls

    C) cannot create sturdy walls   D) can change the texture of cement

5. What can we learn from the last paragraph?

    A) There are many opponents of 3D printing.

    B) Bricklayers in the Netherlands lose their jobs.

    C) The construction industry will be replaced by another industry.

    D) The use of cement harms our environment.

(Text 15)

New York city used to be an early adopter of new transportation modes. In the late eighteen-sixties, New Yorkers took up the velocipede, a primitive version of the bicycle. Half a century later, the city embraced the automobile, and eventually made free parking available for the fossil-fuel burning machines—a remarkable giveaway of expensive public space. New York also engineered and built a subway system, above ground and below ground, which, before the COVID-19 pandemic hit, carried five and a half million riders every weekday—a landmark of American people-moving the city may never reach again, if remote work is here to stay.

But when it comes to shared electric scooters—the adult, motorized versions of the standing "kick" scooter that you push with one foot—New York has taken the slow lane. As with its bike-share scheme, Citi Bike, which launched in 2013, years after most other big cities, New York has adopted a conservative approach to this new mode of getting around town.

Beginning in Southern California, Bird and, later, Lime, both venture-capital-backed tech startups, dropped fleets of rentable electric scooters onto the streets of Santa Monica and San Diego.

Bypassing municipal regulators, the companies hoped to attract customers as quickly as possible. Under Uber's former head of international growth, Travis VanderZanden, Bird got its black-and-white scooters into a hundred cities globally during a yearlong effort.

Although Bird wasn't close to profitable, it soon reached a billion-dollar valuation. Lime then joined Bird. Investors went all in on "micromobility"—the buzzy term for bicycles and lightweight electric vehicles—hoping to stumble onto the next Uber. Within a year, more than thirty scooter-share startups had popped up around the world.

Experts hailed scooter-sharing as the best solution to their "last-mile problem," when the trip between the train station and home is a little farther than walking distance around a quarter of a mile, for most people. Futurists saw it as the first transportation mode to incorporate mobile-computing and global-positioning technology in its core design. They claimed the e-scooter as a predecessor of the battery-powered, software-controlled car of the future. But to critics e-scooters were a fad, and scooter-share programs were a tech hustle that exploited a limited public resource—city streets to enrich private investors.

Among the big transportation hubs in the West, only New York and London stood fast during what is now seen as the scooter mania. Then came the pandemic, scrambling transport habits around the globe, and creating rare opportunities for what transportation theorists refer to as "mode change." To judge from New York's increasingly crowded bike lanes, the scootering mode has arrived.

1. According to Paragraph 1, in the 20th century it was quite unusual for New York to _____.
   A) welcome the arrival of motor vehicles
   B) attract people who didn't possess cars
   C) allow people to park cars free of charge
   D) support the machines powered by battery

2. It can be learned that Bird _____.
   A) leads in the production of scooters
   B) chose San Diego as its first market
   C) has earned more than its overheads
   D) operates in many cities worldwide

3. What does the phrase "stumble onto" (Line 3, Para. 4) most probably mean?
   A) Walk unsteadily.
   B) Encounter by chance.
   C) Nearly fall.
   D) Lose one's way.

4. The criticism of scooter-sharing is that _____.
   A) it is a fashion that will fade away quickly
   B) it will waste the capital from investors
   C) it will exclude bike-sharing from the market
   D) it makes city streets chaotic and unsafe

5. The author's attitude toward scooter-share program is one of _____.
   A) affirmation   B) uncertainty   C) skepticism   D) indifference

(Text 16)

In the small town of Oranmore, on the west coast of Ireland, residents have become used to seeing their morning coffee or evening takeaway descending from the sky and landing, gently, in their front garden. The town is a testbed for Manna, an Irish drone start-up, which can deliver anything from curries and ice cream to books and COVID-19 test kits in minutes to Oranmore's few thousand residents.

Now Manna has raised £18 million to expand into towns in the UK, as its founder believes that drone deliveries will soon become commonplace in much of the country. "The takeaway and delivery market in the UK is larger than the rest of Europe combined," Bobby Healy, who started Manna in 2018, said. "They have 850 million takeaway orders a year. We think that makes the UK absolutely perfect for what we do." Manna said it would be focusing on suburban towns of 50,000 to 100,000 people and planned to open services in the UK by the end of year. It already has a base in Monmouth, where it designs and builds its devices.

For the residents of Oranmore the arrival of drones in October last year was a change. "It's like living in the year 3000," Mary Conroy, 46, a newspaper sub-editor, said. The town's two drones take an average time of three minutes to deliver an item to a customer's door, taking off from the roof of the Tesco supermarket and travelling at about 50mph. The company began testing its drone service in Oranmore last October and offers the service to any retailer or restaurant that wants it, from cafés to bookshops to the pharmacy. It has paired up with Tesco, Just Eat, Samsung and Ben&Jerry's, and has been delivering COVID-19 tests and medicine.

Once at a customer's house, the drone hovers 50m above the houses and then uses sensors to find a suitable flat surface to leave the delivery. The drone then drops down to 15m, at which point hatch doors open and the order is lowered down on a biodegradable rope. The rope detaches once the bag touches the floor and then the drone flies away. The drop on the rope only takes seven seconds but Healy said the system was so adept that customers could order coffee without worrying about any spillage. "We even delivered a cream cake with the candles lit to prove we could do it," he said.

Healy said the company planned to raise more funding, as he believed Manna would need between 40,000 and 50,000 drones to supply a tenth of the UK market.

1. COVID-19 test kits are mentioned in Paragraph 1 to indicate _____.
   A) the hit of the pandemic throughout the world
   B) the importance of disease diagnosis during lockdowns
   C) the success of the tests carried out by Manna
   D) the variety of items the drone could deliver
2. The UK is the targeted market for Manna because _____.
   A) the British like to have their takeaway orders delivered by drones
   B) the British place a massive number of takeaway orders every year
   C) suburban towns have a large population of 50,000 to 100,000
   D) the base in Monmouth allows Manna to fulfill the need of British people
3. What can we learn from Paragraph 3?
   A) In 3000, drones will take over all the deliveries.
   B) Tesco was the first supermarket to use drone delivery.
   C) Residents could get their deliveries very quickly with drones.
   D) Only two drones are used for the delivery in Britain.

4. Which of the following is true of the rope used by the drone?

    A) Its total length must be more than 50 meters.

    B) Its drop must be slow enough to avoid accidents.

    C) It is made of environmentally friendly materials.

    D) It is too sturdy to prevent the spillage of coffee.

5. Which of the following questions does the text answer?

    A) Why did Manna choose Oranmore to conduct the test?

    B) How much money has Manna spent on the pilot project?

    C) Why was a cream cake with the candles lit delivered by drones?

    D) How do drones pick up orders from the supermarket?

(Text 17)

Pulmonologists, emergency responders and intensive-care teams have been the point of the medical spear in battling the COVID-19 pandemic in the U.S. over the past 12 months, but before long, expect another group of specialists to be more engaged than ever: cardiologists. Take a nation that already eats too much, drinks too much, exercises too little and fails too often to show up for regular checkups, put them in lockdown for a year or more, and those behaviors—all of which are drivers of cardiovascular disease—will only get worse.

In a recent survey in the journal *Circulation*, the American Heart Association (AHA) predicted a surge of cardiovascular death and disease in the months and years to come as a lagging indicator of the lifestyle changes forced upon the world by the pandemic. SARS-CoV-2, the virus that causes COVID-19, does on occasion infect and damage heart tissue directly. But in the overwhelming number of cases of coronavirus death, heart failure is not the <u>proximate</u> cause. There's a related truth: the pandemic seems to be leading people into developing the very lifestyle factors that cause heart disease over the long term.

Consider a September 2020 study that showed that alcohol consumption had increased 14% in a sample group of 1,540 adults during the pandemic. Or a study of 3,052 adults showing a decrease in physical activity in 32.3% of adults who were previously physically active. Or the survey conducted by the COVID Symptom Study showing that 31% of adults had reported snacking more during lockdowns.

It's not just eating, drinking and sitting still that can be killers. Elkind and the AHA also cite emotional stress caused by economic hardship, and depression as the isolation drags on. When hospitals and doctors' offices are seen as viral hot zones, people are less likely to show up for routine monitoring of chronic conditions that can have a cardiovascular impact. Acute cardiac events too are being ignored.

In the U.S., about 655,000 people die of heart diseases each year, according to the U.S. Centers for Disease Control and Prevention, a figure that outpaces the 360,000 reported to have died of COVID-19 in 2020. But those statistics don't tell the whole story. Elkind estimates as many as

500,000 additional U.S. deaths in the past year due to people not getting prompt medical help for severe or emergency medical conditions, many of which were cardiovascular in nature.

The good news buried in the bad is that some of the cardiovascular dangers associated with COVID-19 can be controlled. Just as masks mitigate COVID-19 transmission, so can healthier lifestyle choices mitigate heart-disease risks. A pandemic is a severe challenge, but at least some aspects of it can—with effort—be surmountable.

1. Why does the author expect that cardiologists will get busier?
   A) Because there are more drivers who suffer from heart diseases.
   B) Because the new virus prevents people from doing regular checkups.
   C) Because heart diseases may enter a high-incidence period.
   D) Because cardiologists are needed to fight against the pandemic.
2. The word "proximate" (Line 5, Para. 2) is closest in meaning to _____.
   A) special   B) immediate   C) ambiguous   D) fundamental
3. The September 2020 study is cited to show _____.
   A) the formation of unhealthy habits   B) the neglect of heart disease treatment
   C) the mental problems caused by lockdowns   D) the impact of the pandemic on lifestyle
4. It can be learned from Paragraphs 4 and 5 that the COVID-19 pandemic may _____.
   A) lead to more deaths from heart diseases   B) delay the diagnosis of chronic diseases
   C) make patients ignore doctors' suggestions   D) cause psychological problems to decrease
5. Which of the following would be the best title for the text?
   A) Heart Disease: A Big Killer in the Ongoing Pandemic
   B) How to Reduce the Incidence of Heart Diseases
   C) COVID-19 May Lead to a Heart-Disease Surge
   D) The Relation Between Lifestyle and Heart Health

(Text 18)

A Native American community neighboring the only operating uranium mill in the U.S. is hoping a new study will answer longstanding questions about whether it is affecting their health. Members of the Ute tribe say they have seen an alarming increase in health problems in recent years.

The Environmental Protection Agency (EPA) in June gave the approximately 2,000 member tribe a $75,000 grant to design a study that will be conducted with the Centers for Disease Control and Prevention, says Scott Clow, the tribe's environmental director. It will analyze tribal members' health data and environmental conditions to see if any links can be made to the Energy Fuels uranium mill. Results are expected in 2025.

Energy Fuels' facility is also a disposal site for radioactive waste, some of which has been imported from overseas. The company has plans to expand uranium milling as concerns about climate change are increasing demand for carbon free energy, including nuclear.

Contaminants have been confirmed in the local groundwater. The Grand Canyon Trust, an advocacy group, says samples from below the mill have concerning levels of acidity and chemicals. But definitively linking health conditions to environmental contamination is notoriously difficult.

Energy Fuels says the contaminants are nothing to worry about. According to the company, the elements are not significant enough to pose a health risk and the mill takes precautions. For example, radioactive waste is stored in specially-designed ponds called tailing cells. The cells have liners to prevent material from seeping into the ground. Some also have leak-detection systems, but the older cells don't because they were built before the technology was standard. The Grand Canyon Trust says that means it's impossible to know if they're leaking or not.

The Ute Mountain Utes are also worried about air pollution. The water in the tailing cells serves as a barrier that prevents radiation from escaping into the air. But in one 40-acre cell, radioactive material has been left above water for the last two years. The EPA says that's a violation of federal law. The agency says the exposed cell could be emitting up to ten times more radiation than if it were under water, and requires that the mill's radioactive waste remain submerged at all times. In December, the agency told Energy Fuels it must fill the cell.

The company says it's working on it, but filling the cell may take several months because there are limits on how much water at a time can be pumped from wells in the high desert area. "At the end of the day, the Clean Air Act says that that thing should have liquid on it," Clow says.

1. What do we know about the mentioned new study?

   A) It will be subsidized and conducted by the EPA.

   B) It is a large-scale health survey of Americans.

C) It can collect evidence for environment protection.

D) It aims to determine the health impact of the uranium mill.

2. The Grand Canyon Trust seems to believe that _____.

    A) the mill may have polluted the environment

    B) there are some leaks in the older tailing cells

    C) health impact of leakage cannot be determined

    D) Energy Fuels should rebuild its old tailing cells

3. Energy Fuels says the contaminants are nothing to worry about because _____.

    A) the substances in the mill are not harmful to the environment

    B) the leak-detection technology has not reached the standard

    C) safety protection measures are adopted

    D) once the leak occurs, it can be found in time

4. According to the text, the mill's tailing cells _____.

    A) have been in disrepair for years

    B) are not as safe as what the company has asserted

    C) fail to meet the design standard

    D) were made of inferior materials

5. Clow's words are quoted at the end of the text to show that _____.

    A) the mill has violated the Clean Air Act   B) the EPA's judgment may be misguided

    C) Energy Fuels deliberately conceals the fact   D) the health of local residents has been harmed

(Text 19)

As early as 12,000 years ago, nearly three-quarters of land on Earth was inhabited and shaped by human societies, suggesting that global biodiversity loss in recent years may have been driven primarily by an intensification of land use rather than by the destruction of previously untouched nature.

Ellis at the University of Maryland, Baltimore County, and his colleagues analysed the most recent reconstruction of global land use by humans over the past 12,000 years and compared this with contemporary global patterns of biodiversity and conservation. They found that most—72.5 per cent—of Earth's land has been shaped by human societies since as far back as 10,000 BC, including more than 95 per cent of temperate and 90 per cent of tropical woodlands. "Our work confirms that untouched nature was almost as rare 12,000 years ago as it is today," says Ellis. He and his team found that lands now considered intact generally exhibit long histories of use, as do protected areas and lands inhabited by relatively small numbers of indigenous peoples.

The extent of historical human land use may previously have been underestimated because prior analyses didn't fully account for the influence that hunter-gatherer populations had on landscapes, says Ellis. "Even hunter-gatherer populations that are moving around are still interacting with the land, but maybe in what we would see as a more sustainable way," he says.

The researchers also found that in regions now characterised as natural, current global patterns of vertebrate species richness and overall biodiversity are more strongly linked to past patterns of land use than they are with present ones. Ellis says this indicates that the current biodiversity crisis can't be explained by the loss of uninhabited wild lands alone. Instead, it points to recent colonisation and intensification of land use having a more significant role, he says.

"The concept of wilderness as a place without people is a myth," says Yadvinder Malhi at the University of Oxford. "Where we do find large biomes without people living in them and using them—as in North American national parks, Amazonian forests or African game parks—it is because of a history of people being removed from these lands through disease or by force."

Joice Ferreira at Embrapa Amazônia Oriental in Brazil says there are important roles for both protected areas and sustainable land use in preserving biodiversity. "The combination of deforestation, degradation...and climate change make protected areas paramount," she says. "If indigenous custodianship was important in the past, it is much more so nowadays."

1. According to Paragraph 1, the destruction of intact nature _____.
    A) contributes to the modern intensive use of land available
    B) is not to blame for the disappearance of species richness
    C) can be avoided by conventional ways of land development
    D) is caused by the human settlement and other activities

2. One finding discovered by Ellis and his colleagues is that _____.
    A) international efforts are successful in the protection of species richness
    B) the Earth surface has been enlarged by humans for thousands of years
    C) intact nature was restricted to temperate and tropical areas in the past
    D) people had lived in regions that were once considered untouched

3. According to Ellis, hunter-gatherers _____.
    A) did not exert any influence on the land
    B) might exploit the land in a sustainable way
    C) moved around too frequently to interact with the land
    D) were deemed to be of no importance in the past

4. Amazonian forests are mentioned in Paragraph 5 to illustrate _____.
    A) the concept of wildness   B) the universal presence of human beings
    C) the uninhabited wild land   D) why some places are famous

5. It can be learned from the last paragraph that indigenous tribes _____.
    A) play an important role in preserving biodiversity
    B) preserve biodiversity entirely in their own interests
    C) avert climate change and other natural disasters
    D) think the loss of biodiversity a natural thing

(Text 20)

Something is cooking in the world of climate politics. Or, perhaps more accurately, something isn't. This week, the American recipe website Epicurious announced that, for environmental reasons, it wouldn't publish any new beef recipes. No more steaks, burgers or creative ways with mince; no more juicy rib. Since about 15% of global greenhouse gas emissions come from livestock farming, with beef responsible for nearly two thirds of those, it wanted to help home cooks do their bit.

All this seems guaranteed to trigger the sort of people who get very emotional about roast beef and Yorkshire pudding, particularly in the same week that the White House had to quash some wild scare stories about Joe Biden banning burgers to save the planet. But the twist in the tale is that Epicurious actually stopped publishing beef recipes a year ago without telling anyone, and it says its traffic numbers show the vegetarian recipes offered instead were greatly welcomed. Those who scream loudest don't, as ever, speak for everyone.

Cheap and relatively painless ways of tackling the climate crisis are rare, as Boris Johnson may discover once he spells out the detailed implications of Britain's ambitious pledge to cut carbon emissions by 78% by 2035. Swapping gas boilers for environmentally friendly heat pumps will cost thousands, and they won't be suitable for every home. The Treasury, meanwhile, has still yet to rule on the potentially politically toxic question of introducing pay-as-you-go road charges, to replace the fuel tax that the increasing number of electric or hybrid drivers won't be paying. Johnson's preferred green solutions are those that magically allow life to carry on much as before, while new technology does all the heavy lifting—a strategy he described at last week's climate summit as "cake have eat". But that was his Brexit strategy, too, and we've all seen how well that worked out. Dietary changes, however, are one of the few climate change measures where the biggest obstacle to change isn't economic but cultural, and where doing the right thing potentially saves rather than costs individuals money.

Eating habits are already changing, if not fast enough for climate scientists, then faster than angry burger warriors suggest. One in eight Britons claims to be vegetarian or vegan and another one in five flexitarian, eating meat-free sometimes; and although meat consumption rose over the last decade, the big rise was in chicken, not red meat. Going veggie for the sake of the planet, rather than the animals, might have sounded eccentric a generation ago but it barely raises a millennial eyebrow now.

1. According to the text, which of the following is true about beef?
   A) It brings about most of greenhouse gas emissions in livestock farming.
   B) It dominates the recipes published on an American website.
   C) It is the favorite meat ingredient in most household kitchens.
   D) It entails different cooking skills.
2. The decision announced by the website _____.
   A) has caused wild scare stories   B) will reduce the sales of roast beef
   C) will spark the anger of beef-lovers   D) has popularized vegetarian diets
3. The question of introducing pay-as-you-go road charges is mentioned to illustrate _____.
   A) the indecisiveness of British government
   B) the difficulty of conducting eco-friendly measures

C) the impact of Britain's control on greenhouse gas emissions

D) the prospect of electric or hybrid automobiles

4. Dietary changes are expected to _____.

    A) be embraced in some cultures   B) be the focus of scientific research

    C) save money for individuals   D) solve the problems in economy

5. It is indicated in the last paragraph that millennials _____.

    A) are willing to make dietary changes for the sake of the Earth

    B) prefer chicken to red meat

    C) are more selfless than the previous generation

    D) are eager to protect animals

(Text 21)

Rising global temperatures probably contributed to a week of record-breaking heat in Canada and the United States. The devastating heatwave that struck parts of Canada and the United States late last month would have been extremely unlikely without global warming, researchers have concluded. The chance of temperatures in the Pacific Northwest region coming close to 50°C has increased at least 150-fold since the end of the nineteenth century, found a rapid analysis conducted in response to the heatwave.

"This heatwave would have been virtually impossible without the influence of human-caused climate change," says Sjoukje Philip, a climate scientist at the Royal Netherlands Meteorological Institute (KNMI) in De Bilt and a co-author of the analysis. "It was probably still a rare event, but if global warming might exceed two degrees, it might occur every five to ten years in the future." The record-breaking heatwave lasted from 25 June to 1 July, and affected large cities that rarely experience extreme heat, including Portland, Oregon; Seattle, Washington; and Vancouver, Canada.

A group of 27 scientists with the World Weather Attribution (WWA) project rushed to analyse whether global warming had influenced the likelihood of such an intense heatwave occurring in the region.

Their analysis reveals an unambiguous footprint of human-caused climate change. The team compared the observed heat with maximum daily temperatures predicted by climate models, including simulations of temperatures in an atmosphere unaltered by the effect of rising greenhouse-gas concentrations. They concluded that the global average temperature increase of 1.2°C since pre-industrial times made the extreme heatwave at least 150 times more likely to happen.

The analysis was more challenging than similar studies, including those on heatwaves in the past few years in western Europe and Russia, says co-author Geert Oldenborgh, a climate modeller at the KNMI. The peak temperatures observed were up to 5°C higher than previous records in the region. The severity of the heatwave could have been partly due to the effects of earlier drought and unusual atmospheric circulation conditions, he says. It is also possible—although unproven—that climate change is causing local heat extremes to become more frequent and intense than they would be in a cooler climate.

City planners and emergency workers worldwide need to prepare more effectively for the impacts of more frequent heatwaves on human health, agriculture and infrastructure, says co-author Maarten van Aalst, director of the Red Cross Red Crescent Climate Centre in The Hague, the Netherlands. "Heatwaves are topping global disaster death charts, although we are probably missing many cases," he says. "Clearly, local heatwave plans need to be ready for more extreme conditions than in the past."

1. About the record-breaking heatwave, which of the following statements is correct?
   A) It had connection with global warming.
   B) It may cause temperature rise in the Pacific area.
   C) It was only caused by the natural climate change.
   D) It will not happen again in the near future.
2. The research group came to the conclusion by _____.
   A) predicting the possibility of extreme weathers
   B) comparing observed data with simulated ones
   C) analyzing the tendency of climate change
   D) generalizing human influences on climate
3. According to the analysis, the heatwave _____.
   A) will only strike North America   B) may occur intensely and frequently
   C) has caused abnormal atmospheric circulation D) is not the result of earlier drought
4. Mr. Maarten van Aalst calls on the people involved to _____.
   A) explore more ways of urban planning
   B) improve infrastructure for agriculture
   C) cope with the serious consequences of heatwaves
   D) collect all the data about heatwave casualties
5. Which of the following is the theme of the text?
   A) The record heatwave was only caused by human factors.
   B) We must prepare for the adverse effects of droughts.
   C) Heatwave leads to more droughts and unusual air circulation.
   D) Climate change may cause more deadly heatwaves.

(Text 22)

Heatwaves are becoming more common in parts of the United States—and that means more people running their air conditioners for longer. But those air conditioners can make the problem worse, emitting greenhouse gases as they work, which contributes heavily to climate change. SkyCool Systems is trying to break that vicious cycle, using technology that promises to offer buildings an alternative means to cool down by essentially imitating how the planet cools itself.

"Our planet naturally cools itself by sending heat out in the form of infrared light or radiation," said Eli Goldstein, SkyCool's cofounder and CEO, through a process known as radiative cooling.

"We're using that effect to essentially radiate heat out and out during the day and at night, even under direct sunlight."

The five-year-old company said it does this through rooftop panels made using nanotechnology. They resemble solar panels but actually do the opposite, reflecting 97% of the sunlight that hits them and cooling the surface below, according to the company.

A Grocery Outlet store in Stockton, California, which has been using SkyCool's system since last year, says it saw a marked drop in its electrical bills. Jesus Valenzuela, the store manager estimates that the panels have saved his store roughly $3,000 a month.

Scientists have been researching the benefits of radiative cooling for years, but there are some challenges, including a constraint familiar to the solar industry: it doesn't work as well without sunlight. "Our technology works best in hot, dry climates where the sky is clear, so when you have clouds, that blocks that radiative cooling window," Goldstein said.

But perhaps the biggest obstacle to making the technology prevailing is its relatively high cost. Most radiative cooling solutions suffer from a high manufacturing cost and large-scale production limits. Goldstein declined to reveal exactly how much SkyCool's panels cost but acknowledged that they are currently "more expensive" than solar panels. "New technologies like radiative cooling are often more expensive," he said. "People are very sensitive to the cost, and so that is another barrier to getting new things out there."

Much of that is because of low production volumes, he said. Boosting production could help bring the cost down, Goldstein said, particularly for developing countries in Asia and Africa where SkyCool hopes to eventually expand. For now, the company is focused on commercial applications of the technology, though it hopes to start installing panels on the roofs of individual homes. It has installed panels at other locations around California, including a retail store and a data center. "We're just excited to be able to use this new technology for good," Goldstein said.

1. According to the first paragraph, SkyCool's system differs from air conditioners, in that _____.
   A) its cooling technology is more natural   B) its emissions contain greenhouse gases
   C) it may reduce the occurrence of heatwaves   D) it changes the way the atmosphere circulates
2. Which of the following is true of the "radiative cooling"?
   A) It means hiding sunlight.   B) It is the working principle of solar panels.
   C) It is the way the earth cools itself.   D) It needs to rely on nanotechnology.
3. The Grocery Outlet store in California is mentioned to reveal _____.
   A) the popularity of the SkyCool's system   B) the benefit of the SkyCool's system
   C) the necessity of protecting the environment   D) the disadvantages of radiative cooling
4. Mr. Goldstein notes that the SkyCool's system _____.
   A) is about to be put into mass production   B) is costlier than other cooling systems
   C) can finally overcome its technical defects   D) may get popular in developing countries
5. Which of the following would be the best title for the text?
   A) SkyCool's System to Be Put into Trial Operation
   B) Air Conditioners to Be Replaced Before Long

C) Natural Cooling Tech to Cut Electrical Bills

D) New Cooling System Getting the Cold Shoulder

(Text 23)

The European Union could significantly lower carbon emissions by embracing genetically engineered crops. The reason is that GM crops have higher average yields, meaning less land is needed to produce the same amount of food. "That can reduce clearing of new agricultural land," says study co-author Emma Kovak at the Breakthrough Institute in California. "And when land is cleared, that carbon storage is lost."

In fact, according to a 2018 report by the World Resources Institute, if farm yields stay at today's levels, most of the world's remaining forests would have to be cleared to meet estimated food needs in 2050. This would wipe out thousands more species and release enough carbon to warm the world by more than 2℃ , even if all other human emissions stopped, it says.

Kovak and her colleagues have now worked out what the change in carbon emissions would have been if the adoption rates of five key GM crops—cotton, maize, soya beans, rapeseed and sugar beet—had been as high in Europe as they were in the US in 2017, which has a much more favourable view of genetic engineering. The team used data from previous studies to calculate the 33 million tonnes of CO_2 equivalent figure. This represents 8 percent of the EU's total greenhouse gas emissions from agriculture in 2017, so a substantial amount.

Many people think that intensive farming is bad for the environment. If you measure the impact of low-intensity organic farming per area used, it is indeed lower, says Kovak. But per amount of food produced, high-intensity farming has a much smaller impact. "The intensification of farming can spare habitat for wildlife," she says. Tim Searchinger at Princeton University, one of the authors of the 2018 World Resources Institute report, says there is more uncertainty about the yield rises from GM crops than the study suggests. However, the overall evidence does point to yield gains. "I think genetic engineering probably can be very useful," he says.

Luisa Colasimone at the Greenpeace European Unit says genetically engineered crops aren't a good solution. "GE food means handing over food production to a few companies interested only in profits," she says. "GE crops increase the use of harmful chemicals." But some studies have concluded that GM crops have reduced the use of pesticides.

Technologies such as gene editing could produce much more dramatic yield increases in the future. For instance, in 2019, a team boosted tobacco yields by about 40 per cent by fixing a flaw in photosynthesis. This trait is now being engineered into food crops.

1. GM crops can reduce carbon emissions because _____ .

   A) the EU countries didn't grow them in the past

   B) they enhance the carbon storage capacity of land

   C) they reduce the land needed for agriculture

   D) they have the function of storing carbon

2. According to a 2018 report, meeting food demand in 2050 means _____.

    A) a warmer planet   B) a greater biodiversity

    C) zero human emissions   D) large areas of forest

3. We can know from Paragraph 3 that Europe _____.

    A) shares the same attitude to GM crops with the US

    B) has a less favourable view of genetic engineering

    C) contributes to only 8% of global emissions

    D) sustains its population by organic farming

4. Searchinger is quoted to indicate _____.

    A) the uncertainty brought about by GM crops   B) the advantages of intensive farming

    C) the unrealistic result concluded in the report   D) his favourable attitude to genetic engineering

5. Which of the following would be the best title for the text?

    A) The Alarming Situations We May Face in the Year 2050

    B) Intensive Farming Brings More Benefits than Drawbacks

    C) GM Crops Could Greatly Reduce EU Carbon Emissions

    D) Gene Editing Allows Tobacco Yields to Rise Significantly

(Text 24)

No generation should face a future spoiled by a chaotic climate and environmental devastation, yet today's young people do. Their parents benefited from the Great Acceleration—a postwar explosion in human activity with few recent precedents. In the past 50 years, the wealth of millions has increased and the population has doubled. Natural resource extraction has tripled, helping to fuel an almost fivefold increase in the global economy.

Young people have been left to pick up the environmental bill. They live in a world of poisoned rivers, dirty air, razed forests and acidifying oceans polluted by plastic. The UN says 1m of an estimated 8m species of plants and animals are now threatened with extinction. Greenhouse gas emissions are on course to warm temperatures enough to make today's melting ice sheets and extreme weather look like the opening act to a climate tragedy of unthinkable proportions.

All is by no means lost. Despite predictions that the coronavirus crisis would gradually destroy enthusiasm for environmental action, the reverse is happening in many parts of the world. Global investment in renewables and other clean technologies has reached record levels. Countries and companies alike are racing to set net-zero emission targets. Investors are demanding companies clean up their acts.

This is encouraging but inadequate, especially when it comes to the overwhelming threat of global warming. Today's changes in climate systems have occurred because Earth has warmed by an average of just over 1℃ since 1880. To stop that figure rising above 1.5℃, which would bring more climate disruption, scientists say emissions should fall by about 45 percent by 2030 from 2010 levels and reach net zero by around 2050. The pace and scale of action to cut emissions must be radically accelerated.

Since burning fossil fuels for energy is the single biggest source of manmade emissions, and the cost of green alternatives is falling fast, action should start here. A fast phaseout of coal and fossil fuel subsidies is needed, along with other measures to fund for negative emission and protect the forest. Critics urging moderation must remember it has typically taken 50 to 60 years for a large-scale energy transition from one dominant fuel to another. This one must be done in less than 30 years, globally.

Farming accounts for much environmental destruction, and a lot of the climate problem, yet an estimated third of food produced globally is lost or wasted. This wastage will need to end, and surging meat consumption to fall. Persistent recycling and an end to the planned obsolescence of goods must become the norm.

1. The Great Acceleration is mentioned in Paragraph 1 to show that _____.
   A) economic success has come at the expense of environment
   B) the parents of today's young people begin to live better lives
   C) it was easy to make a fortune for parents 50 years ago
   D) the older generation greatly contributed to the global economy
2. What does the underlined phrase "clean up their acts" (Line 5, Para. 3) most probably mean?
   A) Bear the consequence of their behavior.   B) Enhance productivity without pollution.
   C) Stay away from people who misbehave.   D) Improve their behavior or performance.
3. We can learn that emission levels _____.
   A) make it possible to avoid global warming   B) are criticized by scientists for being too radical
   C) should reach net zero by about 2050   D) aim at reaching net zero by around 2030
4. It is inappropriate to make moderate changes because _____.
   A) alternative energy becomes increasingly economic
   B) fossil fuel allowances are a great financial burden
   C) the severity of problems calls for radical measures
   D) the critical situation needs to be addressed quickly
5. It can be learned that the planned obsolescence of goods_____.
   A) offsets the efforts of recycling and reuse   B) accounts for the wastage of most food
   C) should be cancelled   D) stimulates spending during the pandemic recovery

(Text 25)

The Aug. 9 warning from The U.N. Intergovernmental Panel on Climate Change (IPCC) couldn't be more clear: the reality of climate change is unambiguous, its effects are already playing out in every region of the planet, and we need to act now before the outlook gets worse. Today, the effects of climate change are already pervasive; if we continue to emit greenhouse gases at current rates, the effects of climate change will be catastrophic and irreversible.

It's a revelation both shocking to read and perhaps painfully obvious for the countless people who are already feeling the effects—from Germans whose homes were wiped away by floods this year to farmers suffering from ongoing drought in Central America.

The IPCC report, a collaboration among 234 authors, cites more than 14,000 studies and references, covering all the shifts that are occurring in the environment. At the core of all these changes is heat. Global average temperatures have ticked up about 1.1°C since the Industrial Revolution, according to the IPCC, but that seemingly small number obscures the enormous and immediate spikes in temperature in particular places.

Heat waves that bring high temperatures that extend for days have become more frequent, and some areas, particularly vulnerable regions like the Arctic, are warming faster than others. These higher temperatures have a range of ripple effects: an altered jet stream, more intense drought and even increased rainfall, to name a few.

Any one of those ripple effects would create serious problems if it struck on its own, but when multiple ones land at the same time, the result is exacerbated. That's what is happening right now in the Western U.S., where residents are experiencing what the IPCC has called a "compound extreme event."

The U.S. West is not alone in inhabiting very serious climate straits. For the first time, the IPCC this year offered a comprehensive analysis of climate change at the regional level. Every region on the planet has already taken a hit from warming in one form or another, according to the report. In places where people are already facing devastation, the scale of the climate-changed reality is starting to seep in.

Policymakers from around the globe are currently gearing up for global climate talks meant to put the world on track to keep temperatures from rising less than 1.5°C by the end of the century. The IPCC report "will give ammunition to those of us who are saying this is a crisis," says Nat Keohane, president of the Center for Climate and Energy Solutions. But so too should the stories of those on the ground who already have lost homes, livelihoods and loved ones.

1. The warning from IPCC calls on people to _____.
   A) prevent the climate from deteriorating further
   B) look squarely at the reality of climate change
   C) thoroughly explore the causes of climate change
   D) enhance the ability to respond to air pollution
2. The word "spikes" (Line 5, Para. 3) is closest in meaning to _____.
   A) drops   B) decreases   C) increases   D) abnormalities
3. What do we know about the ripple effects in climate?
   A) They are called compound extreme events.   B) They are caused by atmospheric warming.
   C) They mainly affect the Arctic.   D) They usually lead to serious storms.
4. The example of the Western U.S. is used to _____.
   A) analyze regional climate change   B) represent extreme climate events
   C) refute the concept of ripple effects   D) provide evidence for America's development
5. The author's attitude towards the viewpoint of the IPCC is _____.
   A) tolerant   B) skeptical   C) ambiguous   D) supportive

(Text 26)

Founded in 2008 and given European Research Infrastructure Consortium status by the EU Commission in 2015, the Integrated Carbon Observation Systems (ICOS) is a network of 130 carbon-measuring stations set up to measure greenhouse gas concentrations in the atmosphere, as well as how carbon flows between the atmosphere, Earth and oceans. Situated in some of Europe's most remote locations—from far-flung Nordic mountains to French grasslands and Czech wetlands— each station is designed to provide uniform data on carbon emissions across disparate nations and environments.

By making this peer-reviewed data available to scientists and governments worldwide through a centralised portal, ICOS is speeding up our understanding of carbon emissions, and helping scientists keep up with climate change in real time.

ICOS director general Werner Kutsch is actively pushing ICOS to collaborate with researchers from the social sciences, mechanical sciences, behavioural sciences and more behind the climate change banner, in the belief that doing so will help stimulate innovation and help force vital policy change. One of its key developments is in helping governments differentiate between natural and man-made carbon emissions.

Many greenhouse gases occur naturally and are exchanged between the oceans, various ecosystems and the atmosphere. Forests and peatlands, for example, are "sinks", which store carbon dioxide, while forest fires and lakes emit part of it back. Should a sink become significantly weaker—as is currently happening in the Amazon rainforest—Werner believes governments should then be able to use ICOS data to correct the course within a timeframe of months rather than years. The reverse is also possible. Should emissions suddenly decrease, as they have during the global coronavirus pandemic, Kutsch and his team have the chance to see what Earth would look like without the overbearing influence of man.

"We can see that carbon emissions are decreasing through shutting down flights and industries not using as much electricity and so on," says Kutsch. The decrease in emissions coincides with a natural, seasonal decrease that occurs around spring, when more plants remove carbon dioxide through photosynthesis. Kutsch says it should take "some months" for ICOS to collect accurate data on how much of our CO_2 reduction is natural, and how much is a result of the pandemic.

Whatever the data reveals, Kutsch hopes that the current crisis will help governments view climate change differently. "I think this is a learning experience," he says. "Scientists were facing a lot of denial and negative comments in the past, then suddenly we learned from the corona crisis that it is definitely helpful to listen to scientists. I hope this learning experience will last when we're starting to talk about climate change again."

1. What do we know about ICOS?

A) It consists of a great many stations in Europe.

B) It compares atmosphere between land and oceans.

C) It measures greenhouse gas in urban areas.

D) It updates the daily data of climate change.

2. According to Paragraph 3, Kutsch wishes to _____.

A) enable scientists to get information they need

B) promote researchers from related fields to cooperate with ICOS

C) urge the governments' reform and innovation

D) cut down man-made carbon emissions

3. The word "it" (Line 3, Para. 4) refers to _____.

A) greenhouse gas   B) the atmosphere   C) carbon dioxide   D) a "sink"

4. Flight industry is mentioned in Paragraph 5 to _____.

A) explain why there is seasonal carbon emission decrease

B) suggest one of the ways of reducing carbon emissions

C) illustrate how much electricity some industries can use

D) show the impact of human activities on carbon emissions

5. In the last paragraph, Kutsch appeals for _____.

A) verification of the revealed data   B) governments' focus on climate change

C) understanding of learning experience   D) respect for and trust in scientists

(Text 27)

Currently, forests absorb large amounts of carbon dioxide (CO_2) from the atmosphere. This is thought to be due to higher temperatures and abundant CO_2 stimulating growth in trees, allowing them to absorb more CO_2 as they grow. Most earth system models predict that this growth stimulation will continue to cause a net carbon uptake of forests this century. But, the study, led by the University of Leeds and published today in *Nature Communications*, casts doubts on these predictions.

The international study is the largest to date looking at the relationship between tree growth and tree lifespan. The researchers examined more than 200 thousand tree-ring records from 82 tree species from sites across the globe. It confirms that accelerated growth results in shorter tree lifespans, and that growth-lifespan trade-offs are indeed near universal, occurring across almost all tree species and climates. This suggests that increases in forest carbon stocks may be short lived.

Lead author of the study, Dr. Roel Brienen from the School of Geography at Leeds, said: "We started a global analysis and were surprised to find that these trade-offs are incredibly common. It occurred in almost all species we looked at, including tropical trees. Our modelling results suggest there is likely to be a time lag before we see the worst of the potential loss of carbon stocks from increases in tree mortality." They estimate that global increases in tree death don't kick in until after sites show accelerated growth.

The current analysis confirms that, across biomes, reductions in lifespan are not due directly to temperature, but are a result of faster growth at warmer temperatures. Their findings suggests that a prominent cause of the widespread occurrence of a growth lifespan trade-off is that chances of dying increase dramatically as trees reach their maximum potential tree size. Nonetheless, other factors may still play a role as well. For example, trees that grow fast may invest less in defences against diseases or insect attacks, and may make wood of lower density or with water transport systems more vulnerable to drought.

Study co-author Dr. Steve Voelker said: "Our findings, very much like the story of the tortoise and the hare, indicate that there are traits within the fastest growing trees that make them vulnerable, whereas slower growing trees have traits that allow them to persist. Our society has benefitted in recent decades from the ability of forests to increasingly store carbon and reduce the rate at which CO_2 has accumulated in our atmosphere. However, carbon uptake rates of forests are likely to be on the wane as slow-growing and persistent trees are replaced by fast-growing but vulnerable trees."

1. The author introduces the topic of the text by _____.
   A) citing an example   B) raising a question
   C) opposing a viewpoint   D) describing a phenomenon
2. Which of the following best represents the view of Dr. Roel Brienen?
   A) Forests are going to absorb more carbon dioxide.
   B) Carbon stocks may experience a significant loss.
   C) All species of trees are growing faster than before.
   D) Carbon dioxide cannot shorten trees' lifespan.
3. We can infer from Paragraph 4 that fast-growing trees _____.
   A) prefer warmer temperature   B) can better withstand drought
   C) can reach their maximum size   D) may be more vulnerable to diseases
4. The metaphor of "the tortoise and the hare" in Paragraph 5 is used to _____.
   A) emphasize benefits brought by forests   B) explain the fluctuation of carbon stocks
   C) illustrate the merits of fast-growing trees   D) compare trees of different growth speeds
5. Which of the following would be the best title for the text?
   A) Trees Living Fast Die Young   B) Probing into Forest Carbon Stocks
   C) What Is the Net Carbon Uptake? D) A Trade-off between CO_2 and Trees

(Text 28)

Over the past 40 years, temperatures have risen by one degree every decade, and even more so over the Barents Sea and around Norway's Svalbard archipelago, where they have increased by 1.5 degrees per decade throughout the period. This is the conclusion of a new study published in *Nature Climate Change*. "Our analyses of Arctic Ocean conditions demonstrate that we have been clearly underestimating the rate of temperature increases in the atmosphere nearest to the sea level, which has ultimately caused sea ice to disappear faster than we had anticipated," explains Jens Hesselbjerg Christensen, a professor at the University of Copenhagen's Niels Bohr Institute (NBI) and one of the study's researchers.

Together with his NBI colleagues and researchers from the Universities of Bergen and Oslo, the Danish Metrological Institute and Australian National University, he compared current temperature changes in the Arctic with climate fluctuations that we know from, for example, Greenland during the ice age between 120,000-11,000 years ago. "The abrupt rise in temperature now being experienced in the Arctic has only been observed during the last ice age. During that time, analyses of ice cores revealed that temperatures over the Greenland Ice Sheet increased several times, between 10 to 12 degrees, over a 40 to 100-year period," explains Jens Hesselbjerg Christensen.

He emphasizes that the significance of the steep rise in temperature is yet to be fully appreciated. And, that an increased focus on the Arctic and reduced global warming, more generally, are musts.

Climate models ought to take abrupt changes into account. Until now, climate models predicted that Arctic temperatures would increase slowly and in a stable manner. However, the researchers' analysis demonstrates that these changes are moving along at a much faster pace than expected. "We have looked at the climate models analysed and assessed by the UN Climate Panel. Only those models based on the worst-case scenario, with the highest carbon dioxide emissions, come close to what our temperature measurements show over the past 40 years, from 1979 to today," says Jens Hesselbjerg Christensen.

In the future, there ought to be more of a focus on being able to simulate the impact of abrupt climate change on the Arctic. Doing so will allow us to create better models that can accurately predict temperature increases. "Changes are occurring so rapidly during the summer months that sea ice is likely to disappear faster than most climate models have ever predicted. We must continue to closely monitor temperature changes and incorporate the right climate processes into these models," says Jens Hesselbjerg Christensen. He concludes: "Thus, successfully implementing the necessary reductions in greenhouse gas emissions to meet the Paris Agreement on Climate Change is essential in order to ensure a sea-ice packed Arctic year-round."

1. At the beginning of the text, the author uses figures as _____.
   A) the support of his main argument
   B) an introduction to a new research
   C) a comparison with opposed views
   D) the explanation for a phenomenon

2. It can be inferred from Paragraph 2 that _____.
   A) the researchers probed into the history of temperature change
   B) such fluctuations of temperature never appeared before
   C) the temperature during the last ice age was higher than now
   D) Greenland Ice Sheet is the area where temperature rise is the fastest

3. Which of the following statements would Christensen most probably agree with?
   A) Global warming has aroused widespread concern.
   B) Predicted temperature rise is normally different from reality.
   C) The previous climate models should be revised.
   D) UN Climate Panel needs to rethink its research findings.

4. The author ends the text with _____ .

    A) some difficulties of future studies   B) a possible solution to the present problem

    C) an opposing view about the mentioned study   D) an appeal for cooperation of related parties

5. Which of following would be the best title of the text?

    A) The Necessity of Setting up a Climate Model

    B) Temperature Rise and the Environment of the Arctic

    C) It's High Time to Implement the Paris Agreement on Climate Change

    D) The Arctic is Melting Faster than We Thought

(Text 29)

Seeds that float in the air can hitchhike in unusual places—like the air-intake grille of a refrigerated shipping container. A team of researchers from the USDA Forest Service, Arkansas State University, and other organizations recently conducted a study that involved searching for seeds from air-intake grilles over two seasons at the Port of Savannah, Georgia.

The viability of such seeds is of significant interest to federal regulatory and enforcement agencies. Imported refrigerated shipping containers are inspected by the U.S. Customs & Border Protection, Agriculture Program (Department of Homeland Security). The research team worked closely with this agency, as well as the USDA Animal and Plant Health Inspection Service, and the Georgia Ports Authority.

Their findings were recently published in the journal *Scientific Reports*. Seeds from 30 plant species were collected from the air-intake grilles, including seeds of wild sugarcane, a grass on the USDA Federal Noxious Weed List. Federal noxious weeds pose immediate, significant threats to agriculture, nursery, and forestry industries, though wild sugarcane is a lovely grass and useful in its native range.

"During the two shipping seasons, we estimate that over 40,000 seeds from this species entered the Garden City Terminal at the Port of Savannah," says Rima Lucardi, a Forest Service researcher and lead author of the project. "This quantity of incoming seeds is more than sufficient to cause introduction and establishment of this nonnative invader, even if the escape rate from the shipping containers is limited."

To estimate the chance that seeds would survive and establish in the U.S., Lucardi and her colleagues analyzed and modeled viable seeds from four plant species. All are prolific seed producers, wind-dispersed, and able to persist in a wide range of environmental conditions and climates.

The researchers propose several possible strategies for reducing risk to native ecosystems and agricultural commodities. For example, instead of labor-intensive cleaning-up of air-intake grilles, a liquid pre-emergent herbicide could potentially be applied to containers while in port. Prevention and best management practices, from the farm to the store, reduce the probability of nonnative seeds establishing in the U.S. Inspection for exterior seeds hitching a ride on shipping containers at their points-of-origin or stops along the way would also reduce risk of invasion.

Preventing nonnative plant invasions is much more cost-effective in the long run than trying to manage them once they have spread and become widely established. "Investment in the prevention and early detection of nonnative plant species with known negative impacts results in nearly a 100-fold increase in economic return when compared to managing widespread nonnatives that can no longer be contained," says Lucardi.

1. The first two paragraphs enable us to know that _____.
   A) exotic seeds are always floating in the air in unusual places
   B) seeds can be saved in air-intake grilles of shipping containers
   C) the study mainly explored the seasonal transmission of seeds
   D) a few authorities got involved in the hitchhiking seeds project

2. According to the text, wild sugarcane _____.
   A) is usually found in the air-intake grilles   B) can do great harm to the human body
   C) endangers the ecosystem of invaded areas   D) should be imported and effectively used

3. What is the main purpose of this research?
   A) To collect as many exotic plant seeds as possible.
   B) To compare the viability of different plant species.
   C) To study external conditions for the survival of plants.
   D) To stop alien plants from threatening native vegetation.

4. The significance of preventing exotic plants' invasions in advance lies in _____.
   A) the better management of nonnative plants   B) a marked increase in economic efficiency
   C) a complete protection for native species   D) the removal of alien plants' negative impacts

5. The author's attitude towards the mentioned project is one of _____.
   A) full approval   B) severe criticism   C) slight skepticism   D) passive acceptance

(Text 30)

Forecasts aren't just for the weather. Scientists can use weather radar and related technology to chart the journeys of billions of migratory birds, which can help protect them from a growing array of threats. In a new breakthrough on this front, a team led by Colorado State University used millions of observations from 143 weather surveillance radars to evaluate a forecasting system for nocturnal bird migration in the United States.

Using these tools, the team discovered that a mere 10 nights of action are required to reduce risk to 50% of avian migrants passing over a given area in spring and autumn. Specific actions are as simple as turning off nonessential outdoor lights.

The lead author Kyle Horton said that status quo tools for protecting migrating birds are somewhat inefficient. These migrating birds can be negatively impacted by light pollution, wind energy and collisions with structures. "Even during peak migration, it's not efficient to tell people to turn off lights for a period of two to three weeks," Horton said. "Massive numbers of birds migrate on some nights, and at other times, not at all. As scientists, we want to be more mindful about how best to protect migrating birds."

Wind turbines and nighttime lights serve specific purposes for energy production, commercial marketing or public safety. But researchers said with the tools they could predict the most important nights when these global travelers take action. It's easier to identify and encourage specific mitigation strategies.

Migration forecasts are available to the public through Horton's lab website and BirdCast. People can use BirdCast to see daily migration forecasts for the entire United States, as well as location-specific migration alerts. BirdCast scientists, working with state and conservation officials, helped establish a Lights Out Texas initiative and pilot project in late 2020. Nearly one of every three birds migrating through the U.S. in spring pass through Texas, as do one of every four birds migrating through the U.S. in the fall—totaling nearly 2 billion birds.

Mayors in Dallas, Fort Worth and Houston have made commitments to support the new initiative. Former First Lady Laura Bush is also an outspoken advocate, who encouraged Texans to turn off all nonessential lights from 11 p.m. to 6 a.m. during the state's peak spring bird migration, which occurs April 19 to May 7.

Horton said the initiative in Texas will serve as a test bed for other cities across the country. "The same principals equally apply in Denver, Fort Collins, Boulder, New York City or Los Angeles," he said. "These tools are the sort of the thing that agencies or cities and conservation managers can leverage to efficiently guide lights out programs."

1. It is suggested that the Colorado State University team made a breakthrough, in that _____ .
   A) it adopted an innovative technology
   B) it found huge amounts of data
   C) it carried out more extensive observations
   D) it came up with a more specific forecast
2. Which of the following statements is true of Horton's view?
   A) Scientists should find more efficient ways to protect migrating birds.
   B) Current methods to protect migratory birds are out of date.
   C) Migration activities mainly appear in two to three months.
   D) Turning off the lights has no effect on the migration of birds.
3. The phrase "these global travelers" (Line 3, Para. 4) is used to stand for _____ .
   A) the wind turbines   B) the weather radars   C) the migratory birds   D) the bird researchers
4. The author cites the data in Paragraph 5 to emphasize that _____ .
   A) the number of migratory birds is very large
   B) Texas is a key area to protect bird migration
   C) migratory birds only pass through specific areas
   D) BirdCast makes a specific prediction of migration
5. The author ends the text with _____ .
   A) a new research finding
   B) an outlook for future action
   C) some systematic projects
   D) some potential difficulties

Text 31

The United Nations Environment Programme (UNEP) will be 50 next year. But the globe's green watchdog, which helped to create the Intergovernmental Panel on Climate Change (IPCC), very nearly didn't exist.

During talks hosted by Sweden in 1972, low- and middle-income countries were concerned that such a body would inhibit their industrial development. Some high-income countries also questioned its creation. UK representative Solly Zuckerman, a former chief scientific adviser to prime ministers including Winston Churchill, said the science did not justify warnings that human activities could have irreversible consequences for the planet. The view in London was that, on balance, environmental pollution was for individual nations to solve—not the UN.

But the idea of UNEP had powerful supporters, too. India's prime minister, Indira Gandhi, foresaw its potential in enabling industry to become cleaner and more humane. And the host nation made a wise choice in picking Canadian industrialist Maurice Strong to steer the often fractious talks to success. He would become UNEP's first executive director. Two decades later, Strong re-emerged to chair the 1992 Earth Summit in Rio de Janeiro, Brazil, which created three landmark international agreements: to protect biodiversity, safeguard the climate and combat desertification.

UNEP has made some impressive achievements in science and legislation. In 1988, working with the World Meteorological Organization, it co-founded the IPCC, whose scientific assessments have been pivotal to global climate action. It also responded to scientists' warnings about the hole in the ozone layer, leading to the creation of the 1987 Montreal Protocol, an international law to phase out ozone-depleting chemicals.

Strong's successors would go on to identify emerging green-policy issues and nudge them into the mainstream. UNEP has pushed the world of finance to think about how to stop funding polluting industries. It has also advocated working with China to green its rapid industrial growth—including the Belt and Road Initiative to develop global infrastructure. It is essential that this work continues.

UNEP also accelerated the creation of environment ministries around the world. Their ministers sit on the programme's governing council; at their annual meeting last week, they reflected on what UNEP must do to tackle the environmental crisis. Although the environment is a rising priority for governments, businesses and civil society, progress on the UN's flagship Sustainable Development Goals—in biodiversity, climate, land degradation, pollution, finance and more—is next to non-existent. Moreover, the degradation of nature is putting hard-won gains at risk, argues a report that UNEP commissioned.

1. What can we know from the second paragraph?

A) All the high-income countries supported the establishment of IPCC.

B) According to the UK representative, there was scientific evidence for human activities' effect on the earth.

C) Industrial development was a concern for low- and middle-income countries.

D) Representatives from London contended that the UN should be responsible for the global environmental pollution.

2. The author mentioned Maurice Strong in order to _____.

A) illustrate how the talks in Sweden succeeded

B) refute the arguments mentioned in the second paragraph

C) show the determination of the UNEP to found IPCC

D) give an example of supporters of the UNEP

3. UNEP has made an achievement in legislation so as to _____.

A) gradually eliminate the use of chemicals damaging the ozone layer

B) greatly change climate actions all over the world

C) influence the introduction of global laws

D) reduce scientific concerns about global environmental pollution

4. The Belt and Road Initiative of China is mentioned to _____.

A) illustrate the necessity for the business world to make a change

B) argue that UNEP should work hard to achieve more

C) give an example of the action of UNEP

D) show Strong's successors are less capable

5. What would be the author's purpose of writing the last paragraph?

A) To call on policymakers to address the environmental crisis together.

B) To show that there are still a lot for UNEP to do in the future.

C) To explore root reasons why UNEP is not satisfactory.

D) To illustrate the great influence and achievement of UNEP.

(Text 32)

More than 300 businesses have signed an open letter calling on the Biden administration to reduce greenhouse gas emissions in the United States to at least half of 2005 levels by 2030. The signatories include some of largest companies in the United States, including Walmart, Apple, McDonald's and Starbucks. "A bold 2030 target is needed to catalyze a zero-emissions future, spur a robust economic recovery, create millions of well-paying jobs, and allow the U.S. to 'build back better' from the pandemic," the letter said, echoing the president's economic recovery slogan.

Like President Joe Biden's campaign promise to guide the United States to carbon-neutrality by the middle of the century, a 50% reduction target would put the Biden administration in line with what groups such as the United Nations and National Academies of Science say is necessary to mitigate the worst impacts of climate change. It would also require steeper emissions cuts than the country has ever achieved. In 2019, greenhouse gas emissions were approximately 13% below 2005 levels, a decrease of just 1.8% from the previous year.

The Biden administration has identified climate action as one of its top four priorities and has named prominent, experienced Washington insiders, including former Secretary of State John

Kerry and former Environmental Protection Agency (EPA) administrator Gina McCarthy, to oversee climate policy efforts at the White House. Activists on the left are cautiously optimistic about the administration's climate plan after expressing doubts about Biden's climate record during the Democratic primary. New York Democratic Rep. Alexandria Ocasio-Cortez told NPR earlier this month that she feels that Biden has ultimately come around to the side of progressives on climate issues.

The emphasis on climate comes as a sharp departure from the Trump administration, which withdrew the United States from the Paris Agreement and set no emissions reductions targets. Signatories to the Paris deal, which Biden rejoined on the day he was sworn into office, are all required to set these targets—formally known as nationally determined contributions, or NDCs. The agreement also encourages nations to revise their goals every five years, in hopes that the proposals become more ambitious as the cost of environmental reform goes down.

Since the Paris Agreement was first agreed to in 2015, though, just fifty of the deal's nearly 200 signatories have submitted revised targets. A recent U.N. analysis of international climate action found that many countries were doing far too little to reduce emissions for the world to avoid the worst effects of climate change.

So far, the White House has not indicated exactly how ambitious their plan will be. An announcement is expected in the coming days as the White House prepares for its Earth Day climate summit with world leaders, scheduled for Thursday, April 22.

1. According to the first paragraph, the open letter signed by over 300 businesses _____.
   A) expresses firm support for the Biden administration
   B) emphasizes the link between greenhouse gas emissions and economy
   C) appeals for defeating the pandemic all over the U.S.
   D) doubts about the feasibility of the zero-emission target

2. It can be learned from Paragraph 2 that the current administration _____.
   A) faces huge pressure of emission reduction
   B) is severely criticized by the United Nations
   C) is inconsistent with the emission reduction strategy
   D) draws up an improper emission reduction plan

3. The Biden government shows its emphasis on climate by _____.
   A) setting a zero-emission target   B) neglecting the progressives
   C) taking four climate actions   D) nominating some political elites

4. What does the author say about the Paris Agreement in Paragraph 4 and Paragraph 5?
   A) It has exerted little impact on environment protection.
   B) It used to be supported by the Trump administration.
   C) It sets goals that are difficult for nations to achieve.
   D) It is not strictly enforced by some signatory countries.

5. Towards the Biden government's climate action, the author's attitude is _____.
   A) optimistic   B) skeptical   C) wait-and-see   D) let-it-be

Text 33

A tenth of the world's mountain glacier ice will have melted by the middle of this century even if humanity meets the goals of the Paris Climate Agreement, according to figures compiled exclusively for *The Guardian*. The loss is equivalent to more than 13,200 cubic kilometres of water—enough to fill more than 10m Wembley Stadiums—with knock-on effects on highly populated river deltas, wildlife habitats and sea levels.

In some hard-hit areas, including central Europe, North America and low latitudes, glacier mass is expected to decline by more than half. Scientists said the overwhelming bulk of this melt-off, which does not include Greenland or Antarctica, is unavoidable because it has been locked in by the global heating caused by humans in recent years.

However, they say the actions governments take today—including the recent announcements of more ambitious emissions-cutting goals by the US, the UK and others—can make a big difference to the landscape in the second half of this century. "What we see in the mountains now was caused by greenhouse gases two or three decades ago," said the glaciologist Ben Marzeion from the University of Bremen. "In one way, we could see it as a doomsday because it is already too late to stop many glaciers melting. But it is also important that people are aware of how decisions taken now can affect how our world will look two or three generations from now."

Marzeion extracted the data from a synthesis last year of more than 100 computer models generated by research institutes around the world. These studies projected various possible behaviours of the planet's 200,000 mountain glaciers, depending on different emissions pathways and weather circulation patterns. The compiled results are considered the most accurate estimate yet of how mountains will lose their white snowcaps and blue ice-rivers. Marzeion calculated the average mass loss over the various scenarios between 2021 and 2050. It is equivalent to melting almost five Olympic swimming pools of ice every second over the next 30 years.

Aggressive emissions cuts would help to slow this. However, the difference between the best and worst case scenarios was less than 20%. The remaining 80% is already locked in. That contrasts with projections for the second half of the century, when the decisions taken now will make a huge difference. In a low-emissions scenario, current glacier mass is projected to diminish by about 18% by 2100, which would be a slowdown. By contrast, in a high-emissions scenario, the loss would accelerate to reach 36%.

This has a number of consequences. Mountain glacier melt contributes more than a third of sea-level rise, according to the latest European State of the Climate report, which was released last week. This is raising the risk of floods along coastal regions and rivers.

1. The author mentions "more than 10m Wembley Stadiums" in Paragraph 1 to illustrate _____.

   A) the accuracy of the data provided by *The Guardian*

   B) the acreage taken by river deltas and wildlife habitats

   C) the volume of water released by the glacier melt

   D) the public concern about entertainment instead of environment

2. It is indicated in Paragraphs 2 and 3 that it is human behaviour that _____.

    A) indirectly contributes to widespread glacier melt

    B) can change what is happening to glaciers now

    C) can stop the majority of glaciers from disappearing

    D) renders some areas more vulnerable to natural disasters

3. How did Marzeion calculate the mass loss of glaciers?

    A) He took into account different emissions pathways.

    B) He measured the exact area of Olympic stadiums.

    C) He used computer simulation to display the glacier melt.

    D) He took advantage of the studies conducted by research institutes.

4. The author's attitude to aggressive emissions cuts is _____.

    A) pessimistic   B) doubtful   C) supportive   D) indifferent

5. What would be the author's purpose of writing this text?

    A) To illustrate the impracticality of goals set years ago.

    B) To call on the public to respond to global glacier melt.

    C) To explore the root reasons leading to the global warming.

    D) To emphasise the importance of glacier melt research.

(Text 34)

Boris Johnson's government is "too cosy" with vested interests in business to take strong action on the climate crisis, the author of a report on "the polluting elite", has warned.

Peter Newell, a professor of international relations at the University of Sussex, said: "We are never going to have change while these actors are so close to government. The government is not willing to take on these interests as it has close ties to big industries, including fossil fuels." He warned: "The beneficiaries of the status quo are in no rush to change. If we are serious about the Paris Agreement, we have to disrupt that cosy relationship between business and government."

Newell called for more transparency, from party funding to the machinery of government. "A thorough clean-up is needed," he said. "Transparency is needed on where donations go." Prominent figures in international climate action have also revealed to *The Guardian* their concerns that the government's actions on the climate are "uncoordinated", giving a poor impression before the UN climate talks to be hosted by the UK in Glasgow in November.

Newell pointed to the failure to put in place stringent planning regulations that would force house builders to make new homes low carbon. The techniques to do so are available, but add a few thousand pounds to the cost of building a house. Instead, higher costs will have to be borne by the householder when houses built today need to be expensively renovated in a few years' time.

Newell also cited SUVs. Carbon emissions from transport have barely changed in a decade, largely because the savings from people switching to electric vehicles have been wiped out by the sales of SUVs. The government could use the tax system to make SUVs less attractive, but instead has frozen fuel duty for more than a decade and is spending £27bn on new roads, the carbon emissions of which have been grossly underestimated, *The Guardian* has revealed.

Newell was lead author of a report this week from the Cambridge Sustainability Commission that suggested a small number of well-off people—the "polluting elite"—generate far greater emissions than the average UK citizen.

A government spokesperson said: "We all have a part to play in tackling climate change, building on our existing success which has seen us slash emissions over the last three decades faster than any other G7 nation. Through the prime minister's 10-point plan, we have a strategy to eliminate our contribution to climate change by 2050, including ending the sale of new petrol and diesel cars and vans by 2030, and investing in zero emission public transport. "

1. What does Peter Newell think may be a major obstacle to climate action?
    A) The polluting elite.
    B) British government.
    C) The fossil fuels industry.
    D) Close relationship between business and government.
2. By highlighting the "cosy relationship", Newell seems to suggest that _____.
    A) there is a secret financial link between government and business
    B) many social donations are fully open to the public
    C) big businesses consent to the government's strong action
    D) the government refuses to issue a low-carbon development policy
3. House builders are mentioned in Paragraph 4 to present _____.
    A) a background story   B) a contrasting view   C) a supporting case   D) a relevant topic
4. According to *The Guardian*, the sales of SUVs _____.
    A) have been hugely underestimated   B) should have been limited by the tax system
    C) have greatly increased fuel duty   D) have affected the construction of new roads
5. The government's attitude towards Newell's criticism is one of _____.
    A) denial   B) tolerance   C) acceptance   D) indifference

Text 35

In 1923, lead was first added to gasoline to help keep car engines healthy. However, automotive health came at the great expense of our own health and well-being. A new study calculates that exposure to car exhaust from leaded gas during childhood stole a collective 824 million IQ points from more than 170 million Americans alive today, about half the population of the United States.

The findings, from Aaron Reuben, a PhD candidate in clinical psychology at Duke University, and his colleagues, suggest that Americans born before 1996, when leaded gas for cars was banned in the U.S., may now be at greater risk for lead-related health problems, such as faster aging of the brain.

Lead is neurotoxic and can erode brain cells after it enters the body. As such, there is no safe level of exposure at any point in life, health experts say. Young children are especially vulnerable to lead's ability to impair brain development and lower cognitive ability. "Lead is able to reach the bloodstream once it's inhaled as dust, or ingested, or consumed in water," Reuben said. One major way lead used to invade bloodstreams was through automotive exhaust.

To answer the complex question of how leaded gas use for more than 70 years may have left a permanent mark on human health, the researchers opted for a fairly simple strategy. Using publicly available data on U.S. childhood blood-lead levels, leaded-gas use, and population statistics, they determined the likely lifelong burden of lead exposure carried by every American alive in 2015. From this data, they estimated lead's assault on our intelligence by calculating IQ points lost from leaded gas exposure as a proxy for its harmful impact on public health.

The researchers were stunned by the results. As of 2015, more than 170 million Americans had clinically concerning levels of lead in their blood when they were children, likely resulting in lower IQs and putting them at higher risk for other long-term health impairments.

Even more startling was lead's toll on intelligence: childhood lead exposure may have blunted America's cumulative IQ score by an estimated 824 million points—nearly three points per person on average. Dropping a few IQ points may seem negligible, but the authors note that these changes are dramatic enough to potentially shift people with below-average cognitive ability to being classified as having an intellectual disability.

"Millions of us are walking around with a history of lead exposure," Reuben said. "It's not like you got hurt in a car accident and then you're fine. It appears to be an insult carried in the body in different ways that we're still trying to understand but that can have implications for life."

1. The study conducted by Reuben reveals _____.

    A) the link between children's IQ and car exhaust

    B) the rapid popularization of automobile culture

    C) the damage of leaded gas

    D) the causes of brain aging

2. We can learn from Paragraph 3 that lead _____.

    A) can reach bloodstreams

    B) endangers life safety at any time

    C) is most harmful to children

    D) mainly invades brain tissue

3. The researchers reached their findings by _____.

    A) conducting medical experiments

    B) comparing data of varied periods

    C) analyzing relevant statistical data

    D) synthesizing results of the earlier studies

4. In the last paragraph, Reuben emphasized that the effect of lead exposure was _____.

    A) simple   B) long-lasting   C) insignificant   D) strange

5. Which of the following would be the best title for the text?

    A) Reasons for Using Leaded Gasoline

    B) Lead's Harmful Impact on Cars

    C) How Lead Accelerates Aging of Human Brain

    D) Lead Exposure Stealing IQ Scores of Americans

(Text 36)

Researchers at Cornell University have developed a way to help autonomous vehicles create "memories" of previous experiences and use them in future navigation, especially during adverse weather conditions when the car cannot safely rely on its sensors.

Cars using artificial neural networks have no memory of the past and are in a constant state of seeing the world for the first time—no matter how many times they've driven down a particular road before. "The fundamental question is, can we learn from repeated traversals?" said senior author Kilian Weinberger, professor of computer science. "For example, a car may mistake a weirdly shaped tree for a pedestrian the first time its laser scanner perceives it from a distance, but once it is close enough, the object category will become clear. So, the second time you drive past the very same tree, even in fog or snow, you would hope that the car has now learned to recognize it correctly."

HINDSIGHT is an approach that uses neural networks to compute descriptors of objects as the car passes them. It then compresses these descriptions, which the group has dubbed SQuaSH (Spatial-Quantized Sparse History) features, and stores them on a virtual map, like a "memory" stored in a human brain. The next time the self-driving car traverses the same location, it can query the local SQuaSH database along the route and "remember" what it learned last time. The database is continuously updated and shared across vehicles, thus enriching the information available to perform recognition. This information can be added as features to an object detector.

HINDSIGHT is a precursor to additional research (MODEST) the team is conducting, which would go even further, allowing the car to learn the entire perception pipeline from scratch. While HINDSIGHT still assumes that the artificial neural network is already trained to detect objects and augments it with the capability to create memories, MODEST assumes the artificial neural network in the vehicle has never been exposed to any objects or streets at all. Through multiple traversals of the same route, it can learn what parts of the environment are stationary and which are moving objects. Slowly it teaches itself what constitutes other traffic participants and what is safe to ignore. The algorithm can then detect these objects reliably—even on roads that were not part of the initial repeated traversals.

The researchers hope the approaches could drastically reduce the development cost of autonomous vehicles, which currently still relies heavily on costly human annotated data, and make such vehicles more efficient by learning to navigate the locations in which they are used the most.

1. Researchers at Cornell University have developed a way to help self-driving vehicles _____.
   A) utilize their sensors correctly   B) travel on some specific roads
   C) drive in severe weather safely   D) identify objects they have passed by
2. The "memory" of an autonomous vehicle is about _____.
   A) a particular road   B) an object detector
   C) descriptors of objects   D) artificial neural networks
3. Which of the following is correct about HINDSIGHT?
   A) It deletes the SQuaSH data.   B) It upgrades the object detector.
   C) It generates the "memory" content.   D) It corrects errors of the virtual map.
4. MODEST differs from HINDSIGHT in that it _____.
   A) allows the vehicle to learn from scratch
   B) teaches the car to ignore traffic participants safely
   C) utilizes the car's artificial neural network
   D) trains the detector to forget new memory
5. Which of the following would be the best title for the text?
   A) New Algorithm of the Artificial Intelligence
   B) Self-driving Cars Learning from Own "Memories"
   C) To Enhance the Efficiency of Vehicles
   D) Difference Between HINDSIGHT and MODEST

(Text 37)

A rare species of coffee has been found to have a similar flavour to the varieties chosen by coffee growers for their high quality but it is also more tolerant of the higher temperatures and more varied rainfall that are becoming increasingly typical of coffee growing regions.

Many types of coffee beans favoured for their taste only grow in a narrow range of conditions, meaning they might not survive if temperatures increase. In fact, around 60 per cent of wild coffee species are facing extinction. Coffea stenophylla may offer a solution. Farmers stopped cultivating it in the 1920s, believing it couldn't compete in the market at the time, and it was thought to have gone extinct in some countries where it once grew, including Guinea and Sierra Leone. But two small, wild populations were rediscovered in Sierra Leone in 2018.

Historical records showed that the species had an excellent flavour, but Aaron Davis at the Royal Botanic Gardens, Kew in London and his team wanted to test this properly. The researchers created samples of coffee brewed with C. stenophylla beans and served them to five professional judging panels alongside samples of high-quality arabica coffee and robusta coffee, which is commonly used for instant coffee.

The judges said coffee made from C. stenophylla had a complex flavour with sweetness and a good body, similar to the taste of arabica. Some 81 per cent of judges thought C. stenophylla coffee was actually arabica. They also gave it a score of 80.25 on the Speciality Coffee Association's 100-point coffee review scale, meaning it is considered a speciality coffee. "I was really blown away by the taste," says Davis. "It's rare to find something that tastes as good as high-quality arabica, so this is really exciting." C. stenophylla has chemicals in common with arabica, which makes them taste similar. It also contains considerable amounts of kahweol, a substance known for its anti-inflammatory properties.

The team's models, based on what is already known about C. stenophylla, suggest it could tolerate an average annual temperature of around 25℃, which the researchers say is roughly 6℃ higher than arabica. It is also more resistant to varying rainfall, suggesting that C. stenophylla can be cultivated in conditions in which arabica can't.

Davis thinks C. stenophylla has the potential to be commercialised. "It also presents opportunities to breed with other species, like arabica," he says, making them more climate resilient and securing high-quality, high-value coffees for the future. "It's totally the new fashion coffee."

1. The rare breed of coffee _____.
    A) is selected for its unique flavour   B) is a recently-discovered species
    C) is capable of withstanding higher temperatures D) is becoming prevalent in some areas
2. A lot of wild coffee species are dying out because _____.
    A) their taste is not attractive to farmers
    B) they are not hardy to endure temperature changes
    C) they are not competitive in the market
    D) they are replaced by Coffea stenophylla
3. The test on the flavour of C. stenophylla showed that _____.
    A) the judges all favoured the taste of arabica
    B) the result was consistent with previous accounts
    C) the judges were all fascinated by the flavour of C. stenophylla
    D) C. stenophylla contains chemicals in common with robusta

4. What does Davis think of the taste of C. stenophylla coffee?

   A) It's cool.   B) It's hard to describe.

   C) It's odd.   D) It's fantastic.

5. It can be learned from the last two paragraphs that C. stenophylla _____.

   A) offers the possibility to create an adaptable hybrid

   B) meets problems that haven't been tackled to date

   C) has been one of high-quality, high-value coffees for several years

   D) has the potential to dominate the future coffee market

(Text 38)

Americans living in big cities have relatively low rates of depression, despite the hustle and bustle—or maybe because of it, a new study suggests.

Researchers think the pattern can be explained, in part, by the wide range of social interactions that busy cities provide. They developed a mathematical model that predicted big cities would show lower depression rates, based on the varied social interactions residents have—not only with friends, but through work, recreation and even random conversations at the corner coffee shop.

It turned out the prediction was correct: Based on two government health surveys, depression rates were, in fact, lower in large U.S. cities than in smaller ones. The findings do not prove social interactions are the reason, but the researchers accounted for some other possible explanations—like the age of cities' populations, as well as residents' education, income levels and racial makeup. Small cities may have some things going for them—less noise or more green space, for example. But along with small populations, they are often spread out and dependent on car culture. There is no doubt social support can buffer against depression—though the role of incidental, if pleasant, interactions in daily life is unclear.

The new study brings up "important questions" about whether a greater number of social interactions—of all kinds—affect people's depression risk. Dr. Jeffrey Borenstein, president of the Brain & Behavior Research Foundation, agreed that those close relationships with family and friends are vital. More studies, he said, should explore deeply how the environment people live in affects depression risk.

Cities, of course, are not uniform within their limits. People living in a neighborhood that is more isolated or lacking in green space, for example, have a different experience from those in areas filled with parks and easy access to stores, entertainment and other public places. As a next step, the researchers want to see how depression prevalence varies among city neighborhoods.

The current findings do not mean big-city dwellers are "happier" than everyone else. And it's possible that the constant stimulation of urban living is not good for other mental health conditions.

The timing of the data collection is also key: Cities' depression rates were assessed before the COVID-19 pandemic. And COVID may have changed things. Large cities bore the brunt of cases early on—in part, because of all that social connectivity—and pandemic restrictions meant residents were suddenly thrust into an unfamiliar isolation. It would be interesting to see whether the pandemic altered the pattern seen in this study. That could be the "acid test" for the theory that social interactions protect big-city residents from depression.

1. The new study reveals that the reason for the lower depression risk in big cities is _____.
   A) the dull social life
   B) the noisy living environment
   C) the diversified conversation topics
   D) the active interpersonal communication

2. According to Paragraph 3, car culture _____.
   A) is a characteristic of small cities
   B) makes people live separately
   C) makes city residents good at driving cars
   D) may generate more noises

3. About depression risk, Dr. Jeffrey believes that _____.
   A) it does not fully reflect mental health
   B) close relationships with family and friends are essential
   C) it varies among people in different cities
   D) it can be lowered by occasional interactions

4. It can be inferred from the last paragraph that the pandemic _____.
   A) offers the optimum chance to collect data
   B) mainly influences the life in big cities
   C) may challenge the previous conclusion
   D) will increase people's depression risks

5. Which of the following questions does the text answer?
   A) Is social interaction the key to overcome loneliness?
   B) Will the pandemic bring more risks to mental health?
   C) Are the depression rates lower in bigger cities?
   D) Can living environment influence depression risk?

(Text 39)

An international team of scientists compared the main cellular receptor for the virus in humans—angiotensin converting enzyme-2, or ACE2—in 410 different species of animals to predict their risk for contracting the novel coronavirus.

In documented cases of the novel coronavirus infection in mink, cats, dogs, lions and tigers, the virus may be using ACE2 receptors or they may use receptors other than ACE2 to gain access to host cells. Lower trend for binding could translate to lower trend for infection, or lower ability for the infection to spread in an animal or between animals once established.

About 40 percent of the species potentially susceptible to the novel coronavirus are classified as "threatened" and may be especially vulnerable to human-to-animal transmission. Several critically endangered primate species, such as the Western lowland gorilla, are predicted to be at very high risk of infection by the novel coronavirus. Other animals flagged as high risk include marine mammals such as gray whales and bottlenose dolphins. Domestic animals such as cats, cattle and sheep were found to have a medium risk, and dogs, horses and pigs were found to have low risk for ACE2 binding. How this relates to infection and disease risk needs to be determined by future studies, but for those species that have known data, the correlation is high.

Because of the potential for animals to contract the novel coronavirus from humans, and vice versa, institutions including the National Zoo and the San Diego Zoo, which both contributed genomic material to the study, have strengthened programs to protect both animals and humans. "Zoonotic diseases and how to prevent human to animal transmission is not a new challenge to zoos and animal care professionals," said co-author Klaus-Peter Koepfli, a senior research scientist. "This new information allows us to focus our efforts and plan accordingly to keep animals and humans safe."

The authors urge caution against overinterpreting the predicted animal risks based on the computational results, noting the actual risks can only be confirmed with additional experimental data.

Research has shown that the immediate ancestor of the novel coronavirus likely originated in a species of bat. Bats were found to be at very low risk of contracting the novel coronavirus via their ACE2 receptor, which is consistent with actual experimental data. Whether bats directly transmitted the novel coronavirus directly to humans, or whether it went through an intermediate host, is not yet known, but the study supports the idea that one or more intermediate hosts was involved. The data allow researchers to zero in on which species might have served as an intermediate host in the wild, assisting efforts to control a future outbreak of the novel coronavirus infection in human and animal populations.

1. The findings of the research suggest that _____.
   A) ACE2 probably only exists in human bodies
   B) the risk of infection by the novel coronavirus varies across animals
   C) marine life is more vulnerable to the novel coronavirus
   D) the novel coronavirus is usually transmitted from humans to animals
2. The result of this study reveals the importance to _____.
   A) find the species which are at the highest risk of virus infection
   B) call on more research institutions to take part in future studies
   C) prevent human and animal infection by the novel coronavirus with clearer direction
   D) pay attention to the possibility of animal to human infection
3. We can infer from the last two paragraphs that _____.
   A) the result of this analysis may be different from reality
   B) the novel coronavirus originated from the ancestor of bats
   C) the novel coronavirus was transmitted from a bat to a human
   D) all the virus transmission needs several intermediate hosts
4. The phrase "zero in" (Line 6, Para. 6) is closest in meaning to _____.
   A) agree   B) decide   C) remove   D) focus
5. What is the text centered on?
   A) Many animal species may be vulnerable to the novel coronavirus infection.
   B) Scientific research is the key to the prevention of infectious diseases.
   C) Most of mammals are at very high risk of contracting the novel coronavirus.
   D) A method has been found to control the outbreak of the novel coronavirus.

(Text 40)

"Before you criticize a man, walk a mile in his shoes. That way, when you do criticize him, you'll be a mile away and have his shoes."

—Steve Martin

If you imagine that hyper-empathetic Aristotle has a more stressful inner life than shoe-stealing Steve Martin, you're probably right. And that's because you, like Aristotle here, have a functioning emotional intelligence.

Emotional intelligence is a person's ability to accurately perceive, understand, and regulate emotions in oneself and others—sort of like a mood-leveling cocktail of empathy and self-awareness. Having a well-developed EI can be a huge asset in today's increasingly team-oriented workplace, as well as day-to-day social interactions. A strong EI can help make your arguments with loved ones less painful, and connect with strangers in a meaningful way. But for all of this, a new study suggests, there are drawbacks. For starters, it can make you way more stressed.

To test the link between EI and stress, researchers from the Frankfurt School of Finance and Management had 166 male students take a standard EI test that involves identifying emotions on pictured faces and predicting emotional reactions to various scenarios. Following a 20-minute relaxation break, the stress test began. Students were given five minutes to prepare a five-minute speech about their personal strengths and weaknesses as a job candidate, and then asked to deliver it live to one male and one female judge. Five minutes into their speeches, the students were cut off and asked to solve math problems aloud for another five minutes. For those of you who just felt a jolt of anxiety, there is a reason this test has become a scientific standard for measuring stress—even reading about it is painful.

After comparing saliva samples taken before and after the stress test, researchers found this pattern: the students who showed higher emotional intelligence became more stressed during their presentations, and remained stressed for a longer period of time after it was over. Being too empathetic, in other words, can be disabling. This could help explain why the sensation of "feeling embarrassed for someone"—say, everyone onstage during the final moments of the 2017 Academy Awards—can leave you unsettled for the rest of the night.

Naturally, further testing needs to be done to incorporate women and more diverse age groups into our understanding of EI and stress. Until then, simply being self-aware of when your empathy may be kicking into overdrive is an effective way to calm it down. So the next time you feel a secondhand cringe coming on, just breathe deeply, take a step back, and ask yourself, "What would Steve Martin do?"

1. Steve Martin is mentioned as a man who _____.
   A) is not hyper-empathetic   B) likes to criticize others
   C) is under huge pressure   D) behaves improperly
2. According to Paragraph 3, a person with a strong EI can _____.
   A) earn enormous material wealth   B) remove stress from his life
   C) enhance his cognitive ability   D) communicate well with others

3. Which of the following describes the process of the test?

   A) Saliva samples were collected only before the test.

   B) Students had a short break before the stress test.

   C) Students were asked to speak with judges of different genders.

   D) The math problems came after the five-minute speech.

4. The test confirms a viewpoint that _____.

   A) the impact of stress tests may be long-lasting

   B) excessive compassion can be embarrassing

   C) people with a high EI tend to be more stressed

   D) misbehaving on stage may cause uneasiness

5. The author ends the text with _____.

   A) a scheme   B) a question   C) a suggestion   D) some speculation

(Text 41)

He was the King who, according to Shakespeare, "determined to prove a villain." Now geneticists are expected to offer new insights into the appearance and health of Richard III, and even clues to whether he really was inclined to darker personality traits. The complete genome of the last Plantagenet King has been sequenced by scientists led by Professor Turi King, who eight years ago matched DNA from bones discovered at Richard's burial site under a car park in Leicester with that of living relatives.

The genome, which will be published within months, is the first to be sequenced for any leading historical figure. King, of Leicester University's department of genetics and genome biology, said: "It's really interesting and ranges from his blood type to his lactose-intolerance to his genetically inclination to baldness or heart disease." King said that analysis could, among other things, help reveal the genetic basis for his scoliosis—the sideways curvature of the spine revealed in the King's skeleton, which may account for Shakespeare's "hunchback" depiction.

It will provide more detailed information on his likely physical appearance, which has until now been inferred from his skeleton, cruder genetic analysis and a portrait believed to be a Tudor copy of a lost original. Such details could include more detailed and accurate predictions of his likely hair and eye colour, predicted skin tone and any propensity to baldness. Future developments may provide insights into aspects of his facial shape that cannot be precisely inferred from his skull, such as the shape of his nose.

A reconstruction of Richard's face released in 2013 used analysis of his skull and lower-resolution DNA analysis, which suggested that he probably had blue eyes and blond hair that may have darkened as he aged. Intriguingly, scientists are studying possible associations of genes with personality traits, including propensity to violent aggression, psychopathy and narcissism. In future, research may reveal whether Richard carried such genes: the findings would be of great interest, given the debate over whether the King was the evil figure of Shakespeare's depiction or an upright man slandered by Tudor propaganda.

However, King emphasised that this area of genetics remained "extremely fuzzy" and it would take years to <u>tease out</u> any associations. She said that these would never prove one way or the other whether Richard was "horrible" or not, and factors such as his upbringing would also have had a significant effect on personality.

1. It can be learned from Paragraph 1 that Richard III _____.
   A) was the last king of Plantagenet   B) was prone to villainous personality
   C) suffered from some illnesses in his life   D) seemed mysterious to Shakespeare
2. The genetic analysis can provide information on _____.
   A) whether Shakespeare described Richard as "hunchback"
   B) the genome sequence of other leading historical figures
   C) Richard's inclination to baldness
   D) Richard's skull and skeleton
3. It can be inferred from Paragraph 4 that _____.
   A) lower-resolution DNA analysis shows that the King was evil
   B) it is possible that the King was described unrealistically in the past
   C) future research will confirm the aggressiveness of the King
   D) the connection between genes and personality traits is interesting
4. The author's attitude toward genetic research in the text is _____.
   A) optimistic   B) unconvinced   C) neutral   D) sarcastic
5. What does the phrase "tease out" (Line 2, Para. 5) most probably mean?
   A) Succeed in obtaining something through difficulty.
   B) Laugh at people or make jokes about them.
   C) Arouse hope, curiosity or desire.
   D) Tear something into pieces.

(Text 42)

Robots solving computer games, recognizing human voices, or helping in finding optimal medical treatments: those are only a few astonishing examples of what the field of artificial intelligence has produced in the past years. The ongoing race for better machines has led to the question of how and with what means improvements can be achieved. In parallel, huge recent progress in quantum technologies have confirmed the power of quantum physics, not only for its often peculiar and puzzling theories, but also for real-life applications. Hence, the idea of merging the two fields: on one hand, artificial intelligence with its autonomous machines; on the other hand, quantum physics with its powerful algorithms.

Over the past few years, many scientists have started to investigate how to bridge these two worlds, and to study in what ways quantum mechanics can prove beneficial for learning robots, or vice versa. Within an international collaboration led by Philip Walther, a team of experimental physicists have been successful in experimentally proving for the first time a speed-up in the actual robot's learning time. "The experiment could show that the learning time is significantly reduced compared to the case where no quantum physics is used," says Valeria Saggio, first author.

In a nutshell, the experiment can be understood by imagining a robot standing at a crossroad, provided with the task of learning to always take the left turn. The robot learns by obtaining a reward when doing the correct move. Now, if the robot is placed in our usual classical world, then it will try either a left or right turn, and will be rewarded only if the left turn is chosen. In contrast, when the robot exploits quantum technology, the bizarre aspects of quantum physics come into play. The robot can now make use of one of its most famous and peculiar features, the so called superposition principle. This can be intuitively understood by imagining the robot taking the two turns, left and right, at the same time.

"This key feature enables the implementation of a quantum search algorithm that reduces the number of trials for learning the correct path. As a consequence, an agent that can explore its environment in superposition will learn significantly faster than its classical counterpart," says Hans Briegel, who developed the theoretical ideas on quantum learning agents.

This experimental demonstration that machine learning can be enhanced by using quantum computing shows promising advantages when combining these two technologies. "We are just at the beginning of understanding the possibilities of quantum artificial intelligence," says Philip Walther, "and thus every new experimental result contributes to the development of this field, which is currently seen as one of the most fertile areas for quantum computing."

1. We can learn from the first paragraph that quantum technologies _____.
    A) used to be too eccentric for most people to understand
    B) promoted the great development of artificial intelligence
    C) are likely to be applied in the field of artificial intelligence
    D) have emerged to meet people's demands for better life

2. The example of the robot's left-turn learning task is used to demonstrate _____.
    A) the superposition principle   B) features of learning robots
    C) choices of learning paths   D) the magical intuition

3. Why do robots learn faster in the quantum world?
    A) Because they are provided with a simplified learning method.
    B) Because they have first learned the principles of quantum mechanics.
    C) Because they can reduce the number of trials for learning the correct path.
    D) Because they can explore different learning paths at a higher speed.

4. Philip Walther is quoted at the end of the text to _____.
    A) explain theoretical ideas on quantum learning
    B) reveal the limitations of quantum artificial intelligence
    C) predict the future of quantum technology
    D) appeal for more attempts in the new field

5. Which of the following would be the best title for the text?
   A) The Most Fertile Field of Artificial Intelligence
   B) Robots Learn Faster with Quantum Technology
   C) Quantum Technology Makes Amazing Progress
   D) Some New Trials to Improve Learning Robots

(Text 43)

Lockdown has brought noise pollution close to home, whether it is your partner making calls while you are working, or grinding coffee during your Zoom interview. Now research suggests the animal kingdom is also disturbed by the noise of people and their gadgets. Humans have penetrated deeper into wildlife habitats, creating a pervasive rise in environmental sound that not only affects animals' ability to hear, but to communicate. Emerging research suggests noise pollution, for instance by traffic, interferes with animal cognition and mating.

In an attempt to capture the impact of traffic sounds on cognitive performance, researchers gave adult zebra finches—a species of small songbirds native to Australia—a series of foraging tasks. The birds were either in a relatively quiet laboratory environment or subjected to noises designed to simulate a series of cars driving past 20 to 30 metres away.

All tasks, apart from colour association learning, were negatively affected by traffic noise, the researchers reported. The study author, Christopher Templeton said they had not been sure they would see such a strong effect. "These are birds that live in big colonies; they're all talking all the time making quite a big noise. So, to see that just the simple act of hearing cars drive by is enough to really keep them from being able to perform on these tests is pretty surprising."

A separate study, published in the journal *Behavioral Ecology*, looked at how female Mediterranean field crickets made mating choices under different acoustic conditions. Males attract females by performing a courtship song by rubbing their wings together. To test the effect of different noise conditions, the researchers paired female crickets with male crickets whose wings had been clipped to mute their singing skill. The crickets were left to interact in ambient noise conditions, artificial noise conditions, or traffic noise conditions. Then an artificial courtship song was played when the males attempted to court the females.

Females are typically on the hunt for multiple quality males, so the quicker they can mate, the more mates they have, and the more offspring. In the context of ambient noise, the females mounted the males much sooner and more frequently when paired with a high-quality courtship song, the researchers found. But the high-quality song offered no benefit in the white noise and traffic noise conditions, where the females were unable to distinguish the quality of the song. This will have knock-on effects, potentially, to their offspring, and their offspring's viability. But on a population level, mate choices are a really powerful mechanism of sexual selection, and sexual selection drives evolution. Having mate choices disrupted in this way could vastly change the course of evolution.

1. It can be learned from the first paragraph that _____.

    A) lockdown aggravates the pollution of animal habitats

    B) many people use some gadgets to probe into wildlife

    C) human invasion benefits the interaction among animals

    D) the lives of animals are disturbed by human noises

2. Christopher Templeton notes that _____.

    A) noise has little effect on colour cognition

    B) noisy birds are insensitive to ambient sounds

    C) finches are easily frightened by passing cars

    D) the studied birds are more affected by noises than expected

3. In the experiment, the female field crickets were more efficient in mating when they heard _____.

    A) the males singing in a quiet environment

    B) white noise and males singing at the same time

    C) a high-quality artificial courtship song with ambient noise

    D) a high-quality courtship song with traffic noise

4. The study on field crickets' mating choices suggests that _____.

    A) noise pollution made by humans may influence species evolution

    B) females may gradually lose the ability of mate selection

    C) the animals' lifespan relates to the mechanism of sexual selection

    D) environmental noise can damage the course of mate choices

5. What is the main message of this text?

    A) Animals are much more affected by human noises than we have thought.

    B) Research reveals the influence of human noises on animal mating and foraging.

    C) Lockdown brings more noises not only to humans but also to animals.

    D) Noises made by humans will completely change the course of biological evolution.

(Text 44)

Most of the world's 2.22 billion tons of annual trash ends up in landfills or open dumps. Veena Sahajwalla, a materials scientist and engineer at the University of New South Wales in Sydney, Australia, has created a solution to our massive trash problem: waste micro factories. These little trash processors—some as small as 500 square feet—house a series of machines that recycle waste and transform it into new materials with thermal technology. The new all-in-one approach could leave our current recycling processes in the dust.

Sahajwalla launched the world's first waste micro factory targeting electronic waste, or e-waste, in 2018 in Sydney. A second one began recycling plastics in 2019. Now, her lab group is working with university and industry partners to commercialize their patented micro-factory technology. She says the small scale of the machines will make it easier for them to one day operate on renewable energy, unlike most large manufacturing plants. The approach will also allow cities to recycle waste into new products on location, avoiding the long, often international, high-emission treks between recycling processors and manufacturing plants. With a micro factory, gone are the days of needing separate facilities to collect and store materials, extract elements and produce new products.

Traditionally, recycling plants break down materials for reuse in similar products—like melting down plastic to make more plastic things. Her invention evolves this idea by taking materials from an old product and creating something different. "The kids don't look like the parents," she says.

For example, the micro factories can break down old smartphones and computer monitors and extract silica (from the glass) and carbon (from the plastic casing), and then combine them into silicon carbide nanowires. This generates a common ceramic material with many industrial uses. Sahajwalla refers to this process as "the fourth R," adding "re-form" to the common phrase "reduce, reuse, recycle."

In 2019, just 17.4 percent of e-waste was recycled, so the ability to re-form offers a crucial new development in the challenge recycling complex electronic devices. "We can do so much more with materials," says Sahajwalla. "Traditional recycling has not worked for every recycling challenge." She and her team are already working to install the next waste micro factory in the Australian town of Cootamundra by early 2021, with the goal of expanding around the country over the next few years.

1. What does the phrase "leave…in the dust" (Line 6, Para.1) most probably mean?
   A) Render others' efforts futile.　　　B) Leave sb. or sth. far behind.
   C) Improve sb. or sth. greatly.　　　D) Make sth. out of date.
2. According to Paragraph 2, one of the advantages of the new approach is that _____.
   A) it has been in operation since 2018
   B) it has a huge commercial potential
   C) it may utilize sustainable resources in future
   D) it dispenses with the whole process of collection
3. The example of a ceramic material is used to illustrate _____.
   A) new products look the same as the old ones
   B) the products of micro factories can be applied widely
   C) how complex electronic devices can be recycled
   D) something different can be created from an old product
4. It can be inferred that re-form has the potential to _____.
   A) recycle the waste that cannot be recycled with conventional processes
   B) solve all the recycling problems humans may face
   C) bring about changes in the digital manufacturing
   D) gradually take the place of the common 3R phrase
5. Which of the following would be the best title for the text?
   A) The Fourth R　　　　　　　　　B) Waste Micro Factories
   C) Life of Sahajwalla　　　　　　　D) Trash Crisis

Text 45

It was a time when battles, plagues and terrible accidents caused many a misery, but now research suggests the inhabitants of medieval Britain were no strangers to another tribulation: cancer. According to Cancer Research UK around half of people in Britain born after 1960 will receive a diagnosis of cancer during their lifetime. However, such diseases were thought to be relatively rare in medieval times. But experts say an analysis of human bones dating from between the 6th and 16th centuries reveals cancer was about 10 times more prevalent than previously thought.

"It really does highlight that cancer wasn't this really rare disease in the past that most people think of it as being," said Dr Piers Mitchell of the University of Cambridge, a co-author of the study. Writing in the journal *Cancer*, Mitchell and his team report how they carried out inspections, X-rays and CT scans on the remains of 96 men, 46 women and one individual of unknown sex—excavated from six cemeteries in and around Cambridge.

"We had remains from poor people living inside town, we had the rich people living inside town, we had an Augustinian friary inside town and we had a hospital, so we had a real mixture of the different kind of subpopulations that you get in medieval life," Mitchell said, noting that the remains also included those with a farming background.

While the remains span several centuries, Mitchell said the conditions, life expectancy and cancer risks faced by individuals would have been similar, meaning the bones could be taken together for analysis. The team focused on the spine, pelvis and femurs of the remains, Mitchell said, that are the most likely to bear signs of cancer if it has spread to the bones.

The results revealed that five individuals were deemed to have had cancer—with one showing signs of a type of blood cancer. All were middle-aged or older at death. Once the team took into account the proportion of cancers that spread to the bone, as well as the sensitivity of CT scans for picking up signs of such spread, they estimated that between 9% and 14% of the medieval population had the disease when they died. That, the team said, is much higher than the estimate of less than 1% suggested by previous archaeological studies, based on cancer damage visible on the bone surface.

While the research has limitations, Mitchell said the figures could be an underestimate: not all bone types were analysed, while bones affected by cancer may be less likely to survive. The team said the three- to four-fold greater prevalence of cancer now was likely to be down to a range of factors, including the rise in life expectancy and use of tobacco.

1. It was previously believed that in medieval times _____.

   A) British people were not afflicted by wars

   B) 50% of British people had recovered from cancer

   C) people were almost unlikely to have cancer

   D) cancer was more prevalent than it is now

2. X-rays and CT scans are mentioned in Paragraph 2 to show _____.

    A) how reliable the research data is   B) how strict the research procedure was

    C) how the team conducted the study   D) how the team sampled for the study

3. The team mainly studied three parts of the bones because these parts _____.

    A) can be tested together   B) probably show the early signs of cancer

    C) are more likely to stay longer   D) tell different bone types

4. It can be learned from Paragraph 5 that the remains _____.

    A) show five individuals have had cancer in their lifetime

    B) have visible signs of cancer only on bone surfaces

    C) indicate the percentage of cancers affecting bones

    D) belong to individuals who died at a young age

5. According to Paragraph 6, accuracy of the results is partly influenced by _____.

    A) multiple contributing factors like smoking   B) blood types of the excavated remains

    C) the size of bones used in the research   D) the availability of bone types to be studied

(Text 46)

If, as the saying goes, less is more, why do we humans overdo so much? In a new paper featured on the cover of *Nature*, University of Virginia researchers explain why people rarely look at a situation, object or idea that needs improving—in all kinds of contexts—and think to remove something as a solution. Instead, we almost always add some element, whether it helps or not.

The team's findings suggest a fundamental reason that people struggle with overwhelming schedules, that institutions bog down in proliferating red tape, and, of particular interest to researchers, that humanity is exhausting the planet's resources.

"It happens in engineering design, which is my main interest," said Leidy Klotz, Associate Professor in the Department of Engineering Systems and Environment. "But it also happens in writing, cooking and everything else—just think about your own work and you will see it. The first thing that comes to our minds is, what can we add to make it better. Our paper shows we do this to our detriment, even when the only right answer is to subtract. Even with financial incentive, we still don't think to take away."

Klotz, whose research explores the overlaps between engineering and behavioral science, teamed with three colleagues from the Batten School of Leadership and Public Policy on the interdisciplinary research that shows just how additive we are by nature. When considering two broad possibilities for why people systematically default to addition—either they generate ideas for both possibilities and disproportionately discard subtractive solutions or they overlook subtractive ideas altogether—the researchers focused on the latter.

"Additive ideas come to mind quickly and easily, but subtractive ideas require more cognitive effort," the researchers said. "Because people are often moving fast and working with the first ideas that come to mind, they end up accepting additive solutions without considering subtraction at all." The researchers think there may be a self-reinforcing effect. "The more often people rely on additive strategies, the more cognitively accessible they become. Over time, the habit of looking for additive ideas may get stronger and stronger, and in the long run, we end up missing out on many opportunities to improve the world by subtraction."

Klotz has a book that takes a wider view of the topic, *Subtract: The Untapped Science of Less*, coming out a week after the *Nature* paper. Although the timing is coincidence, both the paper and book are products of the interdisciplinary and collaborative research environment at University of Virginia, he said. "It's an incredibly interesting finding, and I think our research has tremendous implications across contexts, but especially in engineering to improve how we design technology to benefit humanity," Klotz said.

1. The study conducted by the researchers of University of Virginia finds that people _____ .

   A) tend to overlook appropriate solutions

   B) are more skilled in additive calculation

   C) prefer to make an improvement by adding something

   D) can't decide if the added thing is useful

2. The word "detriment" (Line 5, Para. 3) is closest in meaning to _____ .

   A) harm   B) mind   C) merit   D) target

3. Which of the following statements would Mr. Klotz most probably agree with?

   A) Engineering is similar to many other disciplines.

   B) Changing a state by adding something is a natural thinking pattern.

   C) Overwhelming schedules are beneficial incentives.

   D) Financial incentive may promote creative thinking.

4. According to the text, what makes people rely on additive ideas?

   A) The habit of quick action.   B) The reluctance to think hard.

   C) The pursuit of improvement.   D) The result of financial stimulus.

5. Which of the following questions does the study try to answer?

   A) How should we free ourselves from stereotypes?

   B) When will our brains turn from addition to subtraction?

   C) How can we do interdisciplinary researches?

   D) Why do we miss opportunities to improve through subtraction?

(Text 47)

If your labrador is not making eye contact, it might not be because it's feeling guilty about wolfing down the biscuits when you weren't looking. It could just be because it's a labrador. A study has found that dogs with longer noses are less likely to look you in the eye. In contrast, those with flatter faces are far more likely to make irresistible puppy dog eyes at you.

In the co-evolution of dog-human relations, eye contact has been a crucial skill. When humans bond, they look each other in the eyes. When dogs became domesticated, they used the same trick to gain our affection. This means that eye contact "plays a fundamental role in dog-human relationships", according to a team of Hungarian scientists writing in the journal *Scientific Reports*.

Past research has shown that holding eye contact raises oxytocin levels in both the dog and its owner, showing its value in bonding for both of them. But we also know that not all dogs are so good at it. As they age, all dogs get less proficient at holding your gaze—either because their visual processing skills diminish or because they just care less. Eye contact skills also seem to vary by breed.

The scientists investigated one factor that might explain it: not the breed itself, so much as the nose length it confers. When a dog has eyes on the side of its head, it can see over a wider range. This is useful in some ways, but what it sacrifices is concentrated focus in the centre of its vision. Such long-nosed dogs are also more likely to be distracted by what is going on around them.

To test this theory, the scientists subjected 130 dogs to a test of eye contact: recording how long it took them to make eye contact with a stranger, and correlating that to the ratio of nose length to head width. A few dogs did not make eye contact at all and had to be excluded. Most, though, managed it. But there was a clear difference. After 15 seconds, about 80 per cent of those with the longest noses had looked the scientist in the eye, compared with 90 per cent of those with the flattest faces. The researchers also found a secondary difference that seemed to depend on the role the dog was bred for. Sheep dogs, bred to follow visual clues, did comparatively better. Dachshunds, bred to follow auditory cues and dive into burrows, did comparatively worse.

The scientists said that it was possible their eye structure explained this difference. It is also possible, though, that our own behaviour did. One of the theories about dogs is that the ones we think are cutest are those that have "hacked" our own evolution—and our tendency to confer affection on things that look childlike, with big eyes.

1. According to the study, a labrador is not looking at your eyes because _____.
   A) it has eaten something sneakily   B) it has a long nose
   C) you are not staring at it   D) it is not willing to do that
2. It is clear that in dog-human relations, _____.
   A) dogs and humans don't evolve together   B) dogs pretend to be human beings
   C) domesticated dogs are very strong   D) eye contact is crucial
3. Which of the following is true of dogs with eyes on the side of their heads?
   A) Their vision is blocked by their noses.
   B) They cannot concentrate on their vision's centre.
   C) Their eyesight is poor.
   D) They are more alert to their surroundings.
4. According to Paragraph 5, the researchers found that _____.
   A) dogs with flat faces were not afraid of strangers
   B) quite a few dogs failed to finish the test
   C) the purpose for which dogs were bred also counts
   D) sheep dogs did well because of their short noses

5. Which of the following might be the best title for this text?

    A) Why Some Dogs Can Hold Your Gaze?   B) Sheep Dogs Are a Much Better Choice

    C) Eye Contact between Dogs   D) Labradors: the Unexpected Thieves

(Text 48)

The US is taking steps to put a nuclear thermal rocket in orbit by 2025, paving the way for improved navigation in space. The Defense Advanced Research Projects Agency (DARPA) plans to turn the long-studied concept of a nuclear thermal rocket into a reality. The technology isn't powerful enough to launch a rocket from Earth, but could provide propulsion for an extended period once in space. This would make it ideal for manoeuvring in orbit or in deep-space missions. "In the air, on the ground and at sea, manoeuvrability is a critical capability," says DARPA project manager Nathan Greiner. "Nuclear thermal propulsion will give us that agility in space."

Such rockets use nuclear power to heat cold propellants to high temperatures, which causes the propellant to expand and provide thrust. The idea for nuclear thermal propulsion was developed by the US Air Force in 1946, as well as by Qian Xuesen at the Massachusetts Institute of Technology in 1947. The engine will run as long as the supply of propellant—typically hydrogen—lasts, which would probably be for a few weeks.

The project will focus on satellites in orbits of up to 400,000 kilometres above Earth, which is far higher than current space operations carried out by military spacecraft. With the technology, military operators could move nuclear-powered communications or spy satellites at will to an area of interest. It could also open up new possibilities, such as tracking and identifying rival stealth satellites. Launching nuclear rockets comes with its own challenges. In 1983, a nuclear reactor on a Soviet spy satellite caused major concern when it malfunctioned and spiralled towards Earth. Fortunately, it burned up harmlessly in the atmosphere as it had been designed to do.

To reduce the risks involved, the DARPA reactor won't be activated until it is in space. "If the reactor hasn't been operated, then it's basically just a quantity of low-enriched uranium," says Laurence Williams, a specialist in nuclear safety at Imperial College London. He says that a detailed safety analysis would still be needed before any launch, looking at what might happen if the rocket failed at lift off or blew up in the atmosphere afterwards.

If the DARPA project succeeds, we could soon see a whole generation of nuclear spacecraft in Earth orbit and beyond. NASA has long been interested in nuclear thermal propulsion for missions to Mars and elsewhere.

1. What can we know from the first paragraph?

    A) A nuclear thermal rocket can be launched directly from Earth.

    B) In the air, the ability to move is more crucial than that on the ground.

    C) Nuclear thermal propulsion is an idea that has been recently proposed.

    D) Nuclear thermal technology allows a spacecraft to move easily.

2. Qian Xuesen is mentioned to illustrate _____.

   A) the origin of a new way to steer spacecrafts

   B) the innovation of nuclear thermal technology

   C) the excellence of Chinese scientists in the US

   D) the support for the technology from the academia

3. It can be inferred from Paragraph 3 that nuclear-powered rockets _____.

   A) have already been applied in deep-space missions

   B) may bring much more powerful military defense

   C) have been pre-programmed to burn up in the end

   D) have been given up because of the Soviet incident

4. The precautions discussed in Paragraph 4 include _____.

   A) using less-radioactive materials for fuel   B) activating the reactor in a proper time

   C) conducting the safety analysis randomly   D) exploding the rocket if malfunction happens

5. The author's attitude to nuclear thermal technology is _____.

   A) cautious   B) ambiguous   C) optimistic   D) indifferent

(Text 49)

Scientists say magic mushrooms' certain component could play an important role in treatment for depression, showing promising results in a clinical trial. Results from the trial have revealed that two doses of psilocybin appear to be as effective as the common antidepressant escitalopram in treating moderate to severe major depressive disorder, at least when combined with psychological therapy. "I think it is fair to say that the results signal hope that we may be looking at a promising alternative treatment for depression," said Dr. Robin Carhart-Harris, a coauthor of the study.

Carhart-Harris said psilocybin was thought to work in a fundamentally different way from escitalopram. Both act on the brain system, he said, but escitalopram seemed to work by helping people tolerate stress more easily, while with psilocybin, it is more about a release of thought and feeling that, when guided with psychotherapy, produces positive outcomes.

Over the six-week trial, 30 out of 59 adults with moderate to severe major depressive disorder were randomly allocated to receive two 25mg doses of psilocybin three weeks apart. The day after the first dose of psilocybin, this group began a daily placebo. The other 29 participants were given two very low, or "inactive", doses of psilocybin three weeks apart. The day after the first dose of psilocybin, this group began a daily dose of escitalopram, the strength of which increased over time.

Each psilocybin session was supervised by at least two mental health professionals. Participants received psychological therapy the day after a psilocybin session, as well as a phone or video call in the week after the first dose.

The results, published in the *New England Journal of Medicine*, reveal that after six weeks both groups showed a similar average reduction in the severity of their depressive symptoms, according to scores from a questionnaire completed by the participants. However, there were other differences. "Psilocybin therapy, as we predicted, works more quickly than escitalopram," said Carhart-Harris.

He added that results from other scales were "suggestive of potential superiority of psilocybin therapy" not only for depression but other aspects of wellbeing.

He warned the findings were not conclusive as the team did not take into account the number of comparisons being made. However, the team noted 57% of patients in the psilocybin group were judged to be in relief of their depression by the end of the six weeks, compared with 28% in the escitalopram group. Neither group had serious side-effects.

1. According to the first paragraph, the clinical trial aims to _____.
   A) develop a new mushroom
   B) test an innovative therapy
   C) study a mushroom ingredient
   D) prove a clinical medical theory

2. Dr. Carhart-Harris believes that psilocybin can help to _____.
   A) adjust the way the brain works
   B) improve the old psychotherapy
   C) release psychological pressure
   D) cultivate positive attitudes towards life

3. During the trial, the psilocybin group of the 30 adults _____.
   A) accepted six weeks of psychotherapy
   B) increased the dosage of psilocybin over time
   C) reported severity of depression
   D) took certain doses of placebo

4. What do researchers think of the effect of the new therapy?
   A) Fairly ideal.
   B) Not perfect.
   C) Still uncertain.
   D) Clearly dissatisfactory.

5. Which of the following would be the best title of this text?
   A) Component of Magic Mushrooms May Help Treatment for Depression
   B) To Release Thoughts and Feelings with Some Experimental Drugs
   C) Probing into New Approaches to Psychological Treatment
   D) What Are the Features of Magic Mushrooms?

第4章 商业经济类

Text 50

The payments frenzy is going global, and Africa is catching the bug. As foreign investment pours in, Africa's fintech firms are expanding both across the continent and into new services. Africa is an obvious choice for fintech investors. They are betting that young African talent can innovate its way out of the region's most pressing financial problems faster than traditional firms can.

By 2025 the continent will be home to 1.5bn people, most of whom will have grown up in the era of the internet. Nigeria, which has received almost two-thirds of Africa's fintech investments this year, has a young and entrepreneurial population. But more than half of Nigerians do not have a bank account. Across the continent, digitally literate unbanked (and underbanked) people, who have long been largely ignored by conventional lenders, are instead turning to the upstarts. In Ivory Coast, for example, 94% of pupils' school fees were being paid using mobile money by 2014. This makes it fertile territory for companies like Wave, which moved into the country in April.

One reason for firms to expand geographically stems from the African Continental Free Trade Area agreement, a deal that was first agreed on in 2018 and which has now been ratified by 38 countries. The Pan-African Payment and Settlement System was launched in September as part of the deal, in order to make the region's many systems work better together.

For the biggest African fintechs, simple payments are only an entry point. OPay was founded three years ago and was once a ride-hailing app. It now offers interest-free credit that is easier for workers in informal jobs to get than bank loans. The firm, now worth around $2bn, is about as valuable as Nigeria's biggest bank. Chipper Cash, which is backed by Jeff Bezos, the founder of Amazon, is taking its vision beyond Africa. It lets Nigerians in Britain send money home instantly, and could revolutionise transfers in sub-Saharan Africa, which has some of the highest remittance costs in the world.

Banks may not be the only incumbents feeling threatened by the newcomers. In some cases telecoms providers, which also provide mobile money, are drastically lowering their fees as competition in payments hots up. The battle leaves regulators struggling to control an industry that is rapidly evolving.

Despite a bumper year, Africa's biggest startups are still relatively young compared with those in the rest of the emerging world. Getting payments right in such a large market could unlock a wealth of opportunity. The emergence of rigorous cross-continental competition this year shows that African fintech is nonetheless maturing, and that the world is at last beginning to pay attention.

1. Why has Africa become a hot spot for fintech investment?

    A) It needs to solve many financial problems.

    B) It is hurt by the global payment frenzy.

    C) It has acquired considerable innovation ability.

    D) It has opened up new areas of financial services.

2. The main customers served by Africa's new fintechs are _____.

    A) university students   B) digital experts

    C) young entrepreneurs   D) unbanked people

3. We can learn from Paragraph 4 that African fintechs _____.

    A) are more popular with low-income people   B) are more convenient than traditional banks

    C) have significantly reduced their service costs D) intend to expand their business in Asia

4. The word "bumper" (Line 1, Para.6) is closest in meaning to _____.

    A) fruitful   B) hard   C) uncertain   D) ordinary

5. The author seems to view African fintechs with _____.

    A) suspicion   B) discontent   C) confidence   D) satisfaction

(Text 51)

It might seem like a logical fix. With domestic gasoline prices surging this month, oil producers could just drill more, right here in the United States. President Biden, who has a complicated history with the oil industry, seems on board. Although his administration is looking to countries such as Saudi Arabia to pump more oil, as well as potentially easing sanctions on Iran and Venezuela, he still believes U.S. oil producers are well equipped to boost production.

Turns out, however, that getting U.S. producers to drill for more oil is easier said than done. Top oil executives warn they won't be able to increase U.S. production anytime soon. Here are some main challenges that U.S. oil producers are facing to boost oil output.

The first challenge is operational. Drilling additional wells is not as simple as turning a spigot and watching oil spill out. U.S. crude production currently stands at 11.6 million barrels per day, according to the latest data from the U.S. Energy Information Administration. That's below March 2020 levels, when the country was producing 13 million barrels per day of crude oil.

The number of workers producing oil and gas had been steadily decreasing since 2015. Then when the pandemic started and demand for oil fell off a cliff, lots of workers were laid off. Employment in the sector dropped from 137,000 workers in February 2020 to 113,000 a year later, according to data from the Bureau of Labor Statistics. Last year, oil and gas producers recovered about half of the jobs lost, but there are still about 12,400 fewer workers producing oil and gas as there were before the pandemic. And that's going to make it harder for oil companies to staff the additional wells needed to pump more oil.

However, the biggest factor for U.S. oil producers may simply be fear. Over the last decade, U.S. oil production saw tremendous growth. But when prices crashed in 2014, investors lost big money. Oil prices are notoriously volatile, with the industry often suffering from boom-and-bust cycles. But in the last few years, investors have been making clear to oil producers that they should not sink money into additional drilling in pursuit of the next oil boom. Instead, they want companies to pay back investors.

Exploration and production companies have responded by recording explosive dividend growth. According to the Morningstar U.S. Market Index, the average dividend in dollars per share has grown from $14 in 2018 to $40 in 2021, an increase of more than 180%. And it's those same investors that may now prevent oil companies from boosting production too much, even as others push for a "drill" approach.

1. It can be inferred from the first two paragraphs that President Biden _____.
   A) feels confident in the increase of U.S. oil output
   B) urges Saudi Arabia to increase oil exports
   C) attempts to stop the rise of domestic oil prices
   D) rejects the proposals of the U.S. top oil executives
2. The operational challenge of boosting oil production is _____.
   A) the high price of drilling wells   B) the insufficiency of oil reserves
   C) the rapid decline in demand   D) the reduction of oil workers
3. The word "volatile" (Line 3, Para. 5) is closest in meaning to _____.
   A) inflated   B) unstable   C) changeless   D) reasonable
4. According to the text, the biggest obstacle to oil production growth comes from _____.
   A) the investors   B) the producers   C) the employees   D) the government
5. The author's attitude to oil output increase in the U.S. is _____.
   A) optimistic   B) hopeful   C) pessimistic   D) indifferent

(Text 52)

A good vegan milk needs to look like milk and taste like milk, and for coffee-drinkers, it should ideally foam like the stuff from a cow. For years manufacturers have had trouble hacking this delicate imitation game. Rapidly rising revenues suggest that they are getting much better at it.

In America alone, $2.6bn of plant-based milk was sold in 2021, up from $2bn in 2018. Pseudo-milks are only one category in the growing assortment of plant-based alternatives to animal products. There are now convincing versions not just of meat but of cheese, eggs and even shrimps. Growing sales show the growing taste for this type of foodstuff. Boston Consulting Group (BCG), a consultancy, reckons that global revenues from alternative proteins could reach $290bn by 2035—and that is a cautious estimate. Eager investors have poured into the business. Alternative-protein companies lapped up $5bn in investments in 2021, 60% more than in 2020. Can the feast last?

One reason to be hopeful is that unlike those early products, which were neither terribly tasty nor particularly nutritious, the latest product is often both tasty and nutritious. Clever processing improves texture, additives boost taste and a pinch of specially engineered peas and beans adds nutrients. Firms are experimenting with ever more novel ingredients in the search for meat- and dairy-like properties that will attract ever more shoppers.

Some are trying to cut saturated fat for health reasons. Fitness fanatics on faddish diets want to develop bulging muscles without building up cholesterol. Concerns about animal welfare and greenhouse-gas emissions from rearing livestock are driving the climate-conscious to limit their animal-derived intake as producing a gram of beef generates 25 times the volume of greenhouse-gas emissions as producing a gram of tofu.

For all the advantages, making a plant not taste like a plant takes work, and ultra-processed substitutes seldom match animal proteins in nutritional value. Plant-based junk food is still junk. Green-minded consumers are realizing that plant-based does not necessarily mean sustainable. Plant-based proteins are also a tough sell in giant markets like India, where diets are already plant-rich, or Nigeria, where meat-eating is a sign of wealth. That limits their global appeal. And animal products, including milk, are better for children's development, though lab-grown versions of meat and dairy are becoming more nutritious.

All this suggests that alternative proteins have far to go to replace the animal kind. The limitations may be weighing on the firms involved. Sales slowed in 2021 and losses widened to $100m in the first quarter of 2022, compared with $27m a year earlier. Plant-based foods may no longer be only an appetiser in diets, but their makers remain one in the food business.

1. Plant-based alternative-protein products are considered to have improved in _____.
   A) texture and flavour
   B) variety and prices
   C) nutrition and intricacy
   D) appearance and effectiveness
2. The phrase "lapped up" (Line 7, Para. 2) is closest in meaning to _____.
   A) withdrew
   B) accepted
   C) demanded
   D) decreased
3. According to the author, some people believe choosing alternative proteins _____.
   A) makes them slimmer
   B) increases their confidence
   C) appears crazier
   D) is more environment-friendly
4. It can be learned from Paragraph 5 that plant-based proteins _____.
   A) can expand its market easily
   B) are regarded as junk food
   C) may not be good enough
   D) stunt children's development
5. The author's attitude toward the prospect of alternative proteins is _____.
   A) cautious
   B) sarcastic
   C) optimistic
   D) ambiguous

(Text 53)

For 27 years Concorde indicated jet-setting glamour. Yet its elegant delta wings came with the ear-splitting noise of thirsty military-derived engines; champagne was served in a cramped cabin with small seats; and cruising at twice the speed of sound, which just about halved the time for an Atlantic crossing, cost twice the regular business-class fare.

"Picking up where Concorde left off" is how Blake Scholl, chief executive of Boom Supersonic, describes Overture 1, the jet which the American startup is developing. It will propel up to 88 passengers 1.7 times as fast as sound while avoiding Concorde's drawbacks. This appeals to United Airlines. On June 3rd it agreed to buy 15 planes, with an option for 35 more. Mr. Scholl promises that supersonic fares, once only for the very rich, will now be "for everyone"—or at least those who can afford to fly business on the same route. Better aerodynamics, materials and engines are intended to keep operating costs 75% below those of Concorde. Civilian engines will propel the aircraft in relative quiet and use sustainable fuel to head off criticism from environmentalists.

United Bank of Switzerland (UBS), a bank, thinks supersonic travel has a future. It puts the cumulative size of the market at between $80bn and $280bn by 2040, depending on regulatory hurdles and whether the planes are delivered on time, on budget and operate as promised. Mr. Scholl is eyeing the upper end of that range, a potential market for 1,200 Overture 1s at $200m each. Then he hopes to make progressively bigger craft offering lower fares and higher speeds. Spike, another American firm with supersonic ambitions, is developing an 18-seat business jet that doesn't make a loud boom.

Is this pie in the sky? For United and for Boom when it seeks more funding, it is unlikely that much cash has yet changed hands. Overture 1 is not set to enter service until 2029. Aerion, another firm that hoped to build an 8-10-seat business jet, unexpectedly folded in May despite orders worth more than $11bn and backing from Boeing, America's giant aeroplane-maker.

National regulations banning supersonic speeds over land rule out trips across North America, home to lots of business travellers and most of the world's business jets. Morgan Stanley, a bank, reckons that at $120m, double the price of a similar subsonic plane, even the ultra-rich wouldn't pay to cut four hours from a transatlantic trip. Tellingly, Boeing itself has no plans to go supersonic. Nor has Airbus, its European main rival. The passenger-jet duopoly reckons that cheaper and cleaner flying is more important than speed. Breaking the sound barrier is still some way off for the ordinary customer.

1. Concord is mentioned in Paragraphs 1 and 2 to present _____.
   A) a topic of harmony   B) a contrasting case
   C) a background story   D) a supporting example
2. Compared with jet aircrafts in the past, Overture 1 improves in the aspect of _____.
   A) air route   B) flying speed
   C) carrying capacity   D) environmental protection
3. The phrase "pie in the sky" (Line 1, Para. 4) is closest in meaning to _____.
   A) unrealistic   B) appealing   C) superior   D) crucial
4. According to the last two paragraphs, which of the following restricts the development of supersonic flight?
   A) Lack of financial support.   B) Unreasonable flight routes.
   C) Legal and regulatory barriers.   D) Limited manufacturing capacity.
5. What does the author think of supersonic flight?
   A) It's hard to reduce its costs.   B) Its prospect is indeterminate.
   C) Its investment risk is too high. D) It's not in line with consumers' wishes.

Text 54

Contractors are facing shortages of building materials as the COVID-19 pandemic disrupts supplies and the construction sector enjoys a boom, squeezing margins and threatening to delay projects. Timber prices have risen more than 80 per cent in the past six months, while copper and steel have jumped 40 per cent, according to the Construction Products Association, a trade body. The warning on rising costs for contractors adds to concerns about inflationary pressures across the global economy, following cautionary messages on rising prices by some of the world's biggest multinationals.

Noble Francis, economics director at the CPA, said the price rises and shortages were "already hitting contractors". He warned that smaller companies were bearing the brunt of the price rises even though they were the least equipped to deal with them as they could not order large quantities in advance and importers were focused on supplying the largest businesses. In an industry in which profit margins average 2-3 per cent, this is a "major risk" despite strong demand, he added.

A shutdown last spring of raw material processing plants followed by a strong global recovery in construction made it difficult to supplement stocks in winter. A quadrupling of shipping costs to record levels in the four months to February has further pushed up costs for shippers, delayed freight deliveries and limited space on ships to send goods. Meanwhile, stay-at-home policies and low borrowing costs across the world led consumers to spend heavily on home improvements and upgrading to bigger houses, resulting in soaring demand for goods and raw materials. That caught out supply chains that had been cutting costs and curtailing production in expectation of a prolonged collapse in demand.

A series of abnormal events from extreme weather to fires at factories have exacerbated shortages of many products. The supply of polymers that are used in construction was affected by the big freeze in February in Texas that shut down as much as 80 per cent of petrochemical production capacity at its peak. Brian Berry, chief executive of the Federation of Master Builders, said 82 per cent of its members were reporting increased prices and struggling to get hold of basic materials such as roof tiles, timber and insulation.

The cost inflation is a black spot in an otherwise positive picture, with the construction industry facing its fastest growth on record. Construction was one of the hardest-hit industries in the first national lockdown, with output falling 41 per cent in April last year. But activity has recovered quickly, boosted by government stimulus for the housing and housebuilding sectors as well as for large projects in the infrastructure sector, such as the high-speed rail project HS2.

1. One cause of the concerns of contractors is _____.

   A) the rising margin of suppliers   B) the thriving construction industry

   C) the pressure from multinationals   D) the large number of projects to be finished

2. According to Francis, small-scale companies are at greater risk because _____.

   A) their equipment is not the most advanced   B) their sensitivity to price changes is low

   C) they lack sufficient storage of materials   D) they fail to import products from overseas

3. What does the author mean by using the phrase "caught out" (Lines 6~7, Para. 3)?

   A) Supply chains became important. B) Supply chains attracted attention.

   C) Supply chains suffered a problem. D) Supply chains surprised consumers.

4. The big freeze in Texas is mentioned to illustrate _____.

   A) the incidents aggravating supply deficiency

   B) the hardest-hit area in the construction industry

   C) the importance of insulation in extreme weathers

   D) the production capacity before the pandemic

5. Which of the following would be the best title for the text?

   A) The Global Craze for House Improvement B) The Grave Mistake Made by Supply Chains

   C) Alarming Situation for Smaller Contractors D) Two Significant Challenges for the Builders

(Text 55)

Since the beginning of the COVID-19 pandemic, industries and businesses across the board have been forced to change working practices and business models in a period of unprecedented global economic uncertainty. How has it affected those working in science, technology, engineering and mathematics (STEM)? That was a key question in this year's *New Scientist* Jobs STEM industry survey, conducted in association with science recruitment specialists. And there is good news: despite the economic setback, science industries and their employees haven't been as hard hit as might be expected, although the future remains uncertain.

More than 2400 people from across industry and academia in Europe and North America took part in the survey. It found that despite COVID-19 uncertainties, salaries for STEM jobs in the UK and North America have increased on average from the previous year, while earnings for the rest of Europe excluding the UK are largely unchanged. The majority of STEM employees feel satisfied in their jobs and are optimistic for the coming year. That said, the pandemic has hindered some people's job plans and prospects. It is no surprise that COVID-19 was seen by survey respondents as their biggest concern over the next 12 months, mentioned by around 40 per cent in all geographical areas covered by the survey.

Lockdowns and other restrictive measures have had a clear and dramatic effect on productivity in the wider economy. According to the UK Office for National Statistics (ONS), economic activity in the country had fallen 30 per cent compared with pre-pandemic levels by May 2020, around two months into the first nationwide lockdown. More than 7 million jobs were considered to be at risk. Dramatic reductions in economic output were also recorded in Europe and the US.

Despite this, UK respondents to the survey this year reported an average salary of £43,424, the highest figure recorded. This places the earnings of survey respondents almost £12,000 above the average of the wider UK workforce. Changes to employment legislation in the UK, for example giving contractors the same pay entitlement as full-time workers, may account for some of this gap, which is also higher than the survey has reported before.

People working in STEM industries are also less likely to have found themselves out of work due to COVID-19. Many countries introduced some form of forced vacation scheme. ONS figures show that in May 2020, when the UK scheme was at its peak, just 14 per cent of people working in the professional, scientific and technical were forced to take their vacations. In the food services and accommodation sector, by comparison, that figure was 80 per cent.

1. The *New Scientist* survey mentioned in the text shows that _____.
   A) STEM industry was not influenced by COVID-19 at all
   B) science industries haven't been affected severely by the pandemic
   C) insecurity and uncertainty abound in the wilder economy
   D) the pandemic is the biggest threat to science industries

2. According to Paragraph 2, which of the following is true of the survey?
   A) Its UK respondents earn more than those in the rest of Europe.
   B) Pharmaceutical sector thrives while other sectors decline.
   C) The pandemic hampers some people's career development.
   D) The majority of STEM employees are worried about COVID-19.

3. The author mentions more than 7 million jobs to illustrate _____.
   A) the influence of lockdowns on economy   B) the prosperity of the UK before the pandemic
   C) the lay-off faced by UK employees   D) the job vacancies after lockdowns

4. One reason for the salary gap between STEM employees and average workers in the UK is _____.
   A) the low income of wider UK full-time workers
   B) the budgetary support for STEM sectors
   C) the secure profits made by STEM contractors
   D) the amendment to employment legislation

5. What can be inferred from the last paragraph?
   A) The unemployment rate of two sectors is higher than that of STEM sectors.
   B) STEM industries received more support from the governments than other sectors.
   C) Workers on vacation maintained their income due to government subsidies.
   D) The jobless people were the fewest when the UK scheme was at its peak.

(Text 56)

Among the records broken at the Tokyo Olympics, one went uncelebrated: the games were the least-watched in decades. In America just 15.5m people tuned in each night, the fewest since NBC Universal began covering the event in 1988. Viewership was 42% lower than at the Rio games in 2016. Broadcasters in Europe recorded similar falls. Yet the Olympics illustrated a puzzle of advertising: Even as audiences desert TV, brands are paying as much as ever for commercials.

Tokyo was an uneven playing field. Many events took place while Americans and Europeans were asleep. COVID-19 meant no spectators, and face-masks all round. But the collapse in viewership wasn't a one-off. Tokyo's opening ceremony was watched by 36% fewer Americans on the day than watched Rio get under way in 2016. Rio's audience in turn was 35% lower than London's in 2012.

The games exemplify a broader trend. This year the average American will watch 172 minutes of broadcast and cable television a day, 100 minutes less than ten years ago, estimates eMarketer, a research firm. Among the so-called "money demographic" of 18- to 49-year-olds, viewership has fallen by half as audiences have gone online. Even so, spending on TV ads is remarkably stable. In 2021 brands will blow $66bn on American commercials, about the same as every year for the past decade.

TV remains "the worst form of advertising, except for all the others", says Brian Wieser of GroupM, the world's biggest ad-buyer. The big streamers, such as Netflix and Disney+, are ad-free zones. Brands are wary of YouTube's user-generated content. As a result, advertisers keep ploughing money into television, even as returns diminish.

Perhaps not for long. YouTube is setting foot in brand advertising as its content mix becomes more professional. Amazon is expected to run ads in its National Football League coverage next year. By combining premium content with targeted commercials, the e-empire is going to unlock "huge buckets" of ad dollars, predicts Andrew Lipsman of eMarketer. In 2019 advertising on streaming services in America was worth only 9% as much as ads on cable and broadcast TV, eMarketer says. In 2023 that figure will be 32%.

Where will this leave events like the Olympics? Probably still "the apple of ad-buyers' eye". Ad money will drain out of daytime and some primetime TV, thinks Mr. Lipsman. But big, live spectacles will be as desirable as ever. There is nothing more powerful in media than the 17 straight days of Olympics dominance. As in sport, it doesn't matter that you aren't as good as you used to be, as long as you beat the competition.

1. Why were the Tokyo Olympic games less-watched?
   A) Because there were unequal competitions in the games.
   B) Because Covid-19 affected the progress of the games.
   C) Because the broadcast time of the games was unreasonable.
   D) Because the audience didn't watch as much TV as before.
2. It can be learned from Paragraph 3 that some people of the "money demographic" _____.
   A) desert TV to browse the Internet   B) keep their steady spending on TV
   C) watch TV for nearly three hours a day   D) prefer watching TV to surfing the Web
3. The word "ploughing" (Line 3, Para. 4) is closest in meaning to _____.
   A) losing   B) wasting   C) investing   D) changing
4. According to eMarketer, advertising on streaming services _____.
   A) will still be hardly accepted by brands   B) will soon replace TV commercials completely
   C) will expand the market in future   D) will improve the quality of ads
5. In terms of Olympic TV broadcasting, the author holds that the media _____.
   A) may become indifferent   B) will still show interest
   C) will get more enthusiastic   D) may raise higher requirements

(Text 57)

In mid-April 2020, the national unemployment rate reached 14.7 percent—the highest since the Great Depression. Forty-one million American workers filed for unemployment between February and May of 2020. Unprecedented unemployment rates don't just have an impact on the unemployed, though. For people still employed during the COVID-19 pandemic, job insecurity and financial concern are associated with greater symptoms of depression and anxiety, according to findings from the School of Nursing in University of Connecticut (UConn) published recently in the Journal of *Occupational and Environmental Medicine*.

The findings are part of a year-long examination of how behavior and social attitudes change, and what factors influence those changes, when people in the United States are faced with the threat of widespread disease. Supported by a National Science Foundation grant, the study is tracking the well-being, feelings, and behavioral practices of about 1,000 individuals across the United States, and more than 18 surveys of the participants have already been conducted since March.

The study asked participants to identify symptoms of anxiety by asking if they were feeling nervous, anxious, or on edge, or if they were not able to stop or control their worrying. They were also asked about the extent of their financial concerns—how worried they were about their employment and financial situation, if they expected their financial situation to get worse over the next 12 months, and if they had the means to secure food and housing for their family for the next 12 months.

Most study participants reported some level of worry about the effects of COVID-19 on their employment. While previous studies have linked large-scale disruptions like recessions and pandemics with poor mental health, the researchers note that their study importantly expands on these associations by demonstrating independent links between greater financial concern with greater anxiety symptoms, and greater job insecurity with greater depressive symptoms, after accounting for demographics, health, and other COVID-19 concerns and experiences.

The researchers say employers can play a critical role in supporting the mental health of their employees by recognizing the increased anxiety that workers experience when their job security feels threatened during the pandemic.

"Our results demonstrate the potential adverse consequences that job insecurity and financial concern have on employees' mental health," the researchers write. "Based on these findings, for those experiencing depressive symptoms during the pandemic, it may be particularly important for employers to be mindful and try to minimize feelings of uncertainty for the employees, as well as instilling hope in employees. For those experiencing anxiety symptoms, employers could attempt to reduce financial concerns by allowing employees to continue to work (eg, telework), even with reduced hours and income, to ensure that employees do not lose their entire income."

1. What do we know from the first paragraph?

 A) The unemployment rate in the United States is at an all-time high.

 B) 41 million people were unemployed in the United States in 2020.

C) The high unemployment rate has little effect on the employed.

D) The employed are also uneasy about their employment prospects.

2. Researchers of the mentioned study mainly asked participants about _____.

    A) their mental conditions   B) their depression symptoms

    C) their views on economic situation   D) their family income and expenditure

3. Through the investigation, the researchers found that _____.

    A) greater economic insecurity can cause serious anxiety

    B) economic development can lead to psychological problems

    C) people infected with COVID-19 are prone to depression

    D) anxiety symptoms are barely associated with physical health status

4. The researchers advised employers to _____.

    A) provide more work opportunities   B) avoid firing their sick employees

    C) make employees feel financially secure   D) allow anxious workers to get fully paid

5. What would be the author's purpose of writing this text?

    A) To call on policymakers to respond to unemployment crisis.

    B) To offer some advice to deal with unemployment anxiety and depression.

    C) To explore root reasons for the rise of unemployment rate.

    D) To illustrate the great influence of pandemics on economy.

(Text 58)

It's being called the world's worst food crisis since the 1970s. Around the globe, food prices have risen about 40% in the last year, sparking protests and violence in at least 14 countries, and pushing the problem to center stage at the United Nations. The rapidly escalating crisis of food availability around the world has reached emergency proportions. Economists blame the runaway prices on an imbalance between the world's supply of food and a recent rise in demand. Demand has been growing rapidly as a result of rapid income growth in many developing countries, especially as you know, in India and some other Asian countries.

Even as the world is eating more, some farmers in the west have turned to growing corn or sugar cane or something other than food to produce fuel. This year, as much as a quarter of the US corn crop will go to ethanol plants reducing the land available to grow food. Grain has also become increasingly valuable on the global market, partly because droughts around the world, especially in Australia, have led to poor harvests.

Other grain-producing countries, such as Argentina and Ukraine have cut back grain exports in a bid to control inflation at home. The result in spikes and cost of food has sparked violent protests in the Caribbean, Africa and Asia. In recent months, Egypt was rocked by two days of riots over high food prices and low wages. Demonstrators took to the streets in Peru, and crowds looted in Somalia. In Haiti, violent protests claimed several lives and cost Haitian Prime Minister Jacques-Edouard Alexis his job. In Vietnam panic shoppers flocked to markets to stock up on rice which rose 100% over a 48-hour period.

Local consumers saw people lining up to buy rice in other countries on TV, so they got in a panic. But Vietnam produces rice. It is impossible to have a rice shortage problem there. Hardest-hit by the food crisis are the world's poor. People in developing countries spend up to 70% of their income on food. So rising prices can quickly lead to hunger. But even in wealthy countries, consumers are feeling pinched.

In the US, many shoppers are clipping coupons and cutting back on luxury items. US food prices next year are forecast to rise about double the increases of recent years. Experts expect world food prices to rise even further. But even when supply and demand find a new equilibrium, few expect prices to drop much, if any, suggesting that more expensive food is here to stay.

1. The rapid rise of food prices _____.
   A) reveals the gravity of the food crisis   B) influences the core work of the UN
   C) leads to a surge in the food demand   D) causes violence in the US
2. In Paragraph 2, the author mainly analyzes the reason why _____.
   A) food prices have risen   B) food demand has decreased
   C) food production has increased   D) cultivated land has increased
3. The author mentioned Vietnam in Paragraph 3 to show that _____.
   A) the grain-producing countries are also short of food
   B) the violent protests there have exerted a profound impact
   C) a panic about food shortage is widespread
   D) the poor suffer the most from water shortage
4. At the end of the text, the author _____.
   A) changes the subject   B) proposes a solution
   C) analyzes the cause   D) makes predictions
5. Which of the following might be the best title for the text?
   A) Serious Impact of Violent Protests
   B) Analysis on the Rise of World Food Prices
   C) Will the World Famine Continue to Spread?
   D) Food Crisis Has Triggered a World Disturbance

(Text 59)

Few leaders at the top of their industries would admit having been mentally pushed to a point where they feared they could not do their job. But Mark Hoplamazian, chief executive of Hyatt Hotels Corporation, the US-based hospitality group, says being honest about his own difficulties during the COVID-19 crisis has only drawn him closer to his colleagues.

"I have to admit to you: I've been through so many stressful periods that I literally couldn't actually access that mindful moment I had come to rely on so much," Hoplamazian, 57, a regular practitioner of meditation, says. "It was costly because at the end of that there is some measure of exhaustion that you feel." Among the darkest times were those when he realised demand at hotels had dropped "to almost zero overnight" and when Hyatt had to let go of hundreds of employees. It was his team that saved him, he says. "I feel like there has somehow been this mutual support network where when I hit a period of time when I was under a tremendous amount of strain…people intuitively or because they are really observant, stepped in."

As for many sectors, the pandemic has precipitated the worst crisis the hotel industry has faced in recent times—perhaps ever. Hyatt, which has a large proportion of its hotels in once desirable but now empty city centre locations, has faced a tougher time than most in the sector. When it announced fourth-quarter results this month it reported a $203m loss, compared with a $164m loss at rival chain Marriott or a $7m loss at Wyndham.

Hyatt owns a greater number of its own hotels than peers such as Hilton and Marriott that tend to operate hotels for property owners under management or franchise contracts and therefore take on less risk. Hoplamazian says that this means Hyatt has been more exposed during the crisis but as a company is more reflective of the distress across the sector. The group cut 1,300 jobs—about 35 per cent of its corporate office workforce—in June.

Hoplamazian says that this has been the toughest year of his career but that he stands by the difficult decision to make job cuts swiftly. "We felt that it was much more humane and respectful if we forced ourselves to make the redundancies early and provide full severance pay and health-care coverage—as opposed to hanging on in the hope that there might be a recall at a later date."

1. What do we know about Mark Hoplamazian?
   A) He has been under tremendous stress during the COVID-19 crisis.
   B) Meditation helps him to relieve the stress from his job.
   C) Being honest is the key to his success as a top leader in the hotel industry.
   D) His job requirements declined sharply due to the pandemic.
2. It can be learned from Paragraph 3 that one result of the pandemic is that _____.
   A) Hyatt sold most of its hotels in the city centres
   B) many bustling downtown areas are no longer crowded
   C) no crisis in the future could have the similar severity
   D) the hospitality industry would be phased out
3. Hyatt is hit the strongest across the sector because _____.
   A) it owns a greater number of franchise contracts
   B) it reflects the hospitality industry
   C) it has the largest corporate office workforce
   D) it doesn't operate more franchise hotels
4. What does the word "redundancies" (Line 3, Para. 5) most probably mean?
   A) Difficulties.   B) Changes.
   C) Layoffs.   D) Concerns.

5. Hoplamazian thinks it is better to _____.

A) maintain the status quo in the difficult situation

B) change his career swiftly

C) force their peers out of business

D) make job cuts as early as possible

(Text 60)

President Biden's pledge to fix the chip shortages hitting auto makers and others will take years to deliver, according to industry officials who are pressing the administration for support as demand for processors continues to soar. Chip-industry executives welcomed Mr. Biden's move but urged patience.

The pandemic supercharged demand for chips that go into everything from videogames and laptops to data centers, products that have become central to remote work and distance learning. Rebounding demand in other industries aggravated the scarcity of chip-production capacity, industry executives said. But that demand surge has caught some industries out, particularly auto makers. General Motors Co., Ford Motor Co. and Volkswagen AG idled some of production capacity as they await critical parts. Car makers are expected to produce around 700,000 fewer cars in the first three months of 2021 than earlier forecast because of chip shortages.

The U.S. semiconductor industry has argued for years that the federal government hasn't sufficiently supported what it says are critical chip-building capacities, including financial inducements to build new plants. The U.S. now accounts for about 12% of global semiconductor manufacturing capacity, down from 37% in 1990 as other countries subsidized growth of their chip makers, according to the Semiconductor Industry Association, a trade group.

Much of the current chip shortage has less to do with where chips are produced than with auto makers and other companies struggling to predict demand for chips—which need long lead-times to produce—during the past year's economic turbulence. Mr. Biden's order on Wednesday calls for a 100-day review in four vital areas, including semiconductors. "We need to stop playing catch-up after the supply-chain crisis hits. We need to prevent the supply-chain crisis from hitting in the first place," the Democratic president said at the signing ceremony.

Jeff Rittener, the head of government affairs at Intel Corp.—the U.S.'s biggest chip maker by sales—said in a blog post that the executive order, coupled with the congressional push to invest, "can help level the playing field in the global competition for semiconductor manufacturing leadership." Intel is weighing more outsourcing of its chip production after manufacturing missteps. Pat Gelsinger, who took over as CEO this month, has said the bulk of the company's chips in the next few years would still be made in house.

Adding U.S. chip-making capacity won't happen overnight. Production facilities cost billions to put up and typically take 18 months or more to start producing integrated circuits, industry analysts say. The push to boost U.S. chip-making capacity comes as demand for those components is expected to remain hot for years. Global chip sales are expected to top $500 billion this year, up around 11% from a year ago, according to research firm Gartner Inc., and grow roughly 18% by mid-decade.

1. Chip-related industries think the U.S. government should _____.

    A) solve the chip shortage as soon as possible   B) maintain moderate growth of chip demand

    C) support the development of chip industry   D) continue to be patient with the chip industry

2. According to Paragraph 2, insufficient chip-making capacity will cause _____.

    A) idle capacity of related industries   B) rapid construction of new plants

    C) fluctuations in chip demand   D) increases in car production

3. What is the main reason for the shortage of chips?

    A) The demand for chips is hard to estimate.

    B) Few factories are capable of producing chips.

    C) The economic turmoil affects chip production.

    D) The government is too strict on the chip industry.

4. Intel's attitude towards Biden's order is _____.

    A) critical   B) sarcastic   C) suspicious   D) favorable

5. Industry professionals predict that the chip industry will _____.

    A) encounter the bottleneck   B) increase chip-making capacity

    C) meet the demands quickly   D) expand capital investment

Text 61

Chancellor Rishi Sunak is to launch a fund that will invest up to £375m of government money in technology companies, and result in the taxpayer taking more stakes in start-ups.

Future Fund: Breakthrough is due to be announced in the Budget on Wednesday and will involve government money being matched by private sector venture capital. The tech sector will be a major focus in the Budget, with Sunak last week saying he would launch a visa scheme to help fast-growing companies recruit high-skilled workers. The fund is meant to support potentially world-beating tech companies that need to scale up to the next stage of development, said people briefed on the plans. These businesses are typically lossmaking, due to the need for big investment in research and development.

The Treasury confirmed the plans, saying the chancellor would co-invest alongside the private sector in "high-growth, innovative UK companies", including those in "life sciences, quantum computing or clean tech". Sunak's fund will risk government money going into companies that fail because the majority of start-ups lose money for their backers. Only a few become global leaders.

A hedge fund investor before going into politics, Sunak has used government money during the pandemic to invest more than £1bn in 1,000 UK start-ups through his Future Fund initiative. That fund, part of the government's COVID-19 business support programme, offered loans to start-ups struggling during the pandemic, with the state money matched by private investors. The government loans can convert into equity stakes, and some already have: the taxpayer is now a shareholder in a toilet maker, a broadband provider and a company that helps make reusable cups.

The new Future Fund: Breakthrough will be aimed at more mature companies with established business models, rather than start-ups hit by the pandemic. It is expected to invest in fewer companies than the Future Fund did. Sunak is a keen proponent of public private co-investment schemes. He has been in talks with Mubadala, the United Arab Emirates-based sovereign wealth fund, about backing a new UK life sciences investment vehicle.

Government officials are also drawing up proposals for a co-investment scheme in Britain's energy sector. Ministers are pursuing several initiatives to woo the tech sector. A report into the financial technology sector by Ron Kalifa, the former Worldpay chief executive, on Friday recommended changes to the listing regime to attract more founder-led businesses to the London Stock Exchange. Another government commissioned report due this week from Lord Jonathan Hill, the former European commissioner, is expected to support listings reform to try to ensure the UK is globally competitive.

1. According to Paragraphs 1 and 2, it is difficult for start-ups to make profit because _____.
    A) the state does not give them sufficient support
    B) taxpayers are reluctant to hold their shares
    C) they cannot hire highly capable employees
    D) they spend a lot money on making technical breakthroughs

2. One possible disadvantage of the government fund is that _____.
    A) it arouses controversy in the government sector
    B) it excludes the participation of private sectors
    C) it may invest in companies that go bankrupt
    D) it encourages some unattainable business goals

3. The example of a broadband provider is used to illustrate _____.
    A) the start-ups that received government fund after the pandemic
    B) the necessary facilities for remote work during the pandemic
    C) the successful conversion of government money into company shares
    D) the only thriving business in the earlier economic downturn

4. The new Future Fund differs from the previous Future Fund in that _____.
    A) it focuses on more mature businesses
    B) it promotes public private co-investment
    C) it backs companies in life sciences
    D) it requires cooperation with foreign funds

5. What is the author's purpose of writing the last paragraph?
    A) To imply the listing regime in the UK is flawed.
    B) To make a brief summary of government efforts.
    C) To suggest the tech sector is the key to UK competitiveness.
    D) To indicate listings reform is inevitable in the near future.

(Text 62)

Tightening labor markets are supposed to make for higher inflation. But at least in the months ahead, the faster the job market recovers, the less serious some inflationary pressures might be.

The Labor Department on Wednesday reported that consumer prices rose 0.4% in February from January, driven by rising gasoline prices. Versus a year earlier, overall prices were up 1.7%, and core prices were up 1.3%. With vaccinations rolling out and another round of government relief landing soon, economists have been raising their inflation estimates.

A fair amount of the increase in inflation will probably come from the simple dynamic of supply struggling to meet demand. As the pandemic hopefully subsides, there will be an unleashing of pent-up demand for services as people go on vacations, take flights to see family and begin eating out at restaurants, again. And thanks to the ample savings many households have built up over the past year—which look as if they are about to be augmented with another round of government support—there will be money to spend. Goods prices could also remain firm, argue Morgan Stanley economists, because inventories are low and supply chain problems persist.

The potential offset to any rise in service prices, in particular, is that after a horrible year a lot of businesses will be interested in selling as much as possible. Restaurants can raise prices if there is a lot of demand, for example, but rather than seeing people lined up out the door, glancing at their watches and leaving, the better option may be to get those diners seated. So building back capacity could be a big focus.

But oftentimes in services sectors, capacity is people. Somebody needs to make the bed, serve the food, cut the hair and tell passengers to put their tray tables up. So businesses will need to hire.

There could be limits on how quickly they can do that. Some are financial: Until more money is actually coming in the door, many small businesses in particular aren't going to bring more people on. Some are logistical: There were about two million fewer people working at restaurants and bars last month than a year earlier, and sorting that many people back into jobs will take time. Complicating matters, a lot of service sector businesses have closed as a result of the pandemic, so getting capacity back to where it was won't be so easy.

Still, despite the hurdles, if demand does pick up, it should be met by an increase in hiring that could, at least in the short run, help alleviate price pressures. Beyond that, of course, the story is different: The faster the job market comes back, the more persistent any increase in inflation will likely be.

1. According to economists, the new round of government support will _____.
   A) push up inflation
   B) lower the prices of goods
   C) boost tourism consumption
   D) solve supply chain problems
2. The example of restaurants in Paragraph 4 is used to _____.
   A) add background knowledge
   B) draw a relevant conclusion
   C) overturn the previous view
   D) analyze causes of low prices

3. What may bring difficulties for businesses to recruit new employees?

A) The shortage of funds.
B) Lack of human resources management.
C) Improper logistical arrangement.
D) Measures to control the pandemic.

4. Which of the following statements is true of the author's judgment on inflation?

A) Inflation could ease with the decrease of commodity prices.
B) The employment rate should rise with inflation in the short term.
C) The picking-up job market may drive inflation higher in the long run.
D) Inflation will cause more unemployment despite the economic recovery.

5. Which of the following would be the best title for the text?

A) Driving Factors of Inflation
B) Problems Caused by the Lack of Supply
C) The Job Market Will Remain Tight
D) Labor Markets Influence Inflation

(Text 63)

The pandemic has led to all sorts of weird economic outcomes. The latest oddity is the growing chorus of complaints in America about a shortage of labour, even though 8m fewer people are in work today than before COVID-19 struck. In early April Bloomberg reported that people are so hard to find that one café in Florida has turned to robots to greet customers and deliver food. The data also back up the anecdote, with total vacancies running at their highest level for at least two decades.

There are three potential explanations for the puzzling shortages: over-generous benefits; fearful workers; and a reallocation of labour between industries. Start with America's huge fiscal handouts. The latest stimulus cheques, posted in the spring, were for up to $1,400 per person. Seemingly every American knows of a neighbour's cousin's boyfriend who received a cheque, then quit his job in order to sit on the sofa. Economic research has long concluded that more generous benefits decrease incentives to look for work.

Yet this relationship appears to have weakened during the pandemic. The fact that increases in Unemployment Insurance payments have been time-limited may make workers reluctant to turn down a job with longer-lasting rewards. This suggests that the second factor, fear, may be important in explaining America's shortage of staff. Nearly 4m people are not looking for work "because of the coronavirus pandemic", according to official data. Jobs in health care, recreation and hospitality report the highest level of job openings. By contrast, in industries where maintaining social distancing or being outside is often easier, labour shortages are less of an issue. The number of job openings per employee in the construction industry is lower today than it was before the pandemic.

The final reason for worker shortages relates to the extraordinary reallocation of resources under way in the economy. The general growth in vacancies represents the rise in opportunities in some industries—say, clerks in DIY stores—as others decline, reflecting changing consumer demands. Analysis by *The Economist* of over 400 local areas also finds a wide variation in job markets across geographies: the gap between jobs growth in the most buoyant areas and that in struggling ones is twice as wide as it was before the pandemic.

As vaccinations continue to reduce hospitalisations and deaths from COVID-19, and limit the spread of the disease, Americans' fears about taking high-contact jobs should fade too. But if shortages are to dissipate fully, and the threat of inflation is to be contained, some of the unemployed will also have to take up work in sectors and areas that are new to them.

1. The "latest oddity" (Line 1, Para. 1) refers to _____.

   A) growing complaints about the employment situation in the U.S.

   B) the coexistence of unemployment increase and labor shortage

   C) the sharply increasing number of job vacancies

   D) serious difficulty in recruiting new employees

2. The example of a neighbor's cousin's boyfriend is mentioned to show _____.

   A) people's indifference to government handouts

   B) the insufficient amount of benefits

   C) the generosity of America's fiscal handouts

   D) the small effect of benefits

3. People's worry about the pandemic directly led to _____.

   A) a serious employment situation   B) the increase of government relief

   C) the shrinking demand for employees   D) the uneven distribution of labor force

4. It can be learned from the last two paragraphs that the labor problem _____.

   A) is caused by the growth of consumption demand

   B) may lead to severe inflation in the long run

   C) appears quite different in varied regions

   D) can be solved with the control of the pandemic

5. In this text, the author attempts to explain _____.

   A) why workers are hard to find when unemployment is high

   B) what may be a possible effect of government relief

   C) how the problems in the U.S. labor market can be solved

   D) who will be affected by the reallocation of economic resources

第5章　教育文化类

(Text 64)

Josiah Pena spent many hours staring at a computer screen for online classes during his senior year at San Jose State University, and he was facing even more screen time when he landed a remote internship in 2020. That's when he decided to order blue-light-blocking eyeglasses on Amazon. They soothe eye fatigue, some reviews said. They are snake oil, some doctors warned.

At least most people agree on one thing: They make you look really hot. Mr. Pena thinks the glasses help with screen fatigue, but even if that's not backed by science, the glasses are worth the $25 price.

Aimee Abel, 28, a brand strategist, bought a two-pack shortly before the pandemic on Amazon. She says she wears them when she wants to shift her mind-set to be more focused during work time or as an accessory whenever she wants to be taken seriously, such as during meetings with clients. "I see myself in glasses and I'm like, 'There's a professional. She's an expert in her field. She's gonna be giving thoughtful responses.'" says Ms. Abel.

Sunir Garg, the clinical spokesperson of the American Academy of Ophthalmology, says that humans are more exposed to blue light from the sun than they are from devices, and that there isn't enough research to prove that blue light causes eye damage. "Over time, the eye has done a great job evolving to filter out the harmful effects of sunlight, and that includes blue light, so that's kind of myth No. 1," says Dr. Garg.

Kala Sanders, a first-grade teacher, says her students often complained about how much their eyes hurt from looking at their computer screens. So she, along with several other teachers across the country, started fundraisers through Donors Choose, a funding website for teachers, to get all of their students blue-light glasses. She was sold on them after finding online research that said they could help with better sleep. She and some parents also noticed less complaining by the students about eye fatigue while wearing them, says Mrs. Sanders.

Blue-light exposure at night can impede natural melatonin production, making it difficult to fall asleep after spending hours scrolling through Instagram. Dr. Garg says that for some people who struggle with falling asleep, they could potentially be helpful, but for the majority of people "it is not worth spending money on." Even though they are looking at the world through the dream-colored glasses, some users can see where the doctors are coming from. "I do think it's a gimmick," says Ms. Abel, "and I'm OK with that."

1. Josiah Pena bought blue-light-blocking eyeglasses to _____.

    A) complement his face   B) relieve brain fatigue

    C) look fashionable   D) protect his eyes

2. Aimee Abel emphasizes her glasses' effect on _____.

    A) facial expression

    B) creative thinking

    C) psychological hint

    D) interpersonal relationship

3. Dr. Garg points out that blue light _____.

    A) will not lead to eye damage

    B) may cause dreaminess at night

    C) can be separated from sunlight

    D) will not make people sleepless

4. According to Kala Sanders, blue-light glasses _____.

    A) were received by her students

    B) used to help her improve sleep

    C) are going to be donated to teachers

    D) enabled her to gaze at screens longer

5. What is Abel's attitude towards wearing blue-light glasses?

    A) Critical.   B) Supportive.   C) Skeptical.   D) Negative.

(Text 65)

A hot course at Harvard Business School (HBS) promises to teach future leaders an elusive skill—managing happiness. As business schools train the corporate chieftains of tomorrow, skills like emotional awareness and improving well-being are taking their places alongside deal making and financial modeling. Courses on happiness, relationships and balance are among the most in-demand courses at top MBA programs. Their popularity reflects both the demand for soft skills and students' desire for more-balanced lives—and an intention among schools to turn out better bosses.

At Harvard, the 180 spots in Arthur Brooks' "Leadership and Happiness" fill up quickly. Participants are taught how to cultivate their teams' happiness, along with their own. Happiness isn't just a product of chance, genes or life circumstances, Dr. Brooks posits, but of habitually tending to four key areas—family, friends, meaningful work, and faith or life philosophy.

The course was first offered in the spring semester of 2020, intersecting with the arrival of COVID-19. Happiness at work has since taken on new urgency for employees and managers, as workers leave jobs at record rates and rethink their goals. A social scientist who joined Harvard in 2019 after leading the conservative-leaning American Enterprise Institute for a decade, Dr. Brooks said he sometimes felt lonely as a boss and was inspired to pitch the class to Harvard after observing the same with other leaders.

Dr. Brooks' students take assessments of their relationships, materialistic values and other emotional metrics. Some high achievers, he said, rank highly on finding meaning and accomplishments but score lower on positive emotions. "You're deferring your gratification constantly," he said, which can lead to burnout.

That resonated with Ashley McCray, an engineer and consultant in the class. She recalled being named to a 2019 list of top women in business in Minneapolis and St. Paul—but focusing on the next goal instead of enjoying the accomplishment. She now serves as the appointed HBS Student Association's "Vice President of Happiness," sharing happy moments from around campus on social media and helping classmates recharge with campus therapy dogs and massages.

Mark Giragosian, a 2021 HBS graduate working in a private equity, now stores a series of tips for daily practice in his office desk drawer, reminding him to stay aware of future goals but live in the present. That guidance is especially helpful when things go wrong, he said. Mr. Giragosian advises stressed associates to fix mistakes, then move on and not be overwhelmed by things they can't change. The course has also helped him understand his own fear of failure. People don't fear failure itself, Dr. Brooks tells students, but how failure will make them feel.

1. According to the first paragraph, courses about happiness managing are _____.
   A) preferred by better bosses   B) attracting a lot of attention
   C) now compulsory for the executives D) replacing traditional courses
2. In his course teaching, Dr. Brooks _____.
   A) focuses on people's fear of failure B) gives tips for workplace happiness
   C) finds out the defects of high achievers D) reveals the related factors of happiness
3. What prompted Dr. Brooks to offer this course?
   A) His academic stand and beliefs.   B) The trend of social development.
   C) His feeling of loneliness.   D) The requirement of Harvard leaders.
4. The example of Ashley McCray is used to show that _____.
   A) people should live in the present
   B) high achievers often have long-term goals
   C) happiness needs to be shared among friends
   D) a balance should be kept between work and rest
5. Mark Giragosian advises people not to _____.
   A) be afraid of failure   B) forget their mistakes
   C) pay attention to future objectives D) be obsessed with the unchanged things

Text 66

I have three kids under 10 who don't expect—or even want—to play with me. It took some practice, but over time, we've all learned we're better off doing our own thing: the kids, without stodgy parental interference, and my husband and I, unhooked from the assumption that we have to play to be present.

In the past, if they couldn't agree on a game's direction, I would try to help, only to make it worse: when Mom is there to listen, they turn defensive and mean. I know I'm lucky they have each other to play with, and so I've taught myself to hold back. I tell myself they're learning about compromise and boundaries. As am I. My motto is "Moms don't play." Our third child joined the family with this system in place, and he is, as most third children are, remarkably independent.

I can't say that my approach is right for everyone. I know that it resonates for me in part because of how I was raised. I have no memories of my parents playing with me. I can remember reading together and their swimming with me in the ocean, but they weren't involved in the fashion shows I filmed with my sisters, and they didn't help me make my magazine, *Kid Stuff*, either. Not once did they dine at my fictional restaurant.

This isn't a complaint; it's gratitude. They may not be a part of these memories, but they weren't absent either. They were on the edges—there but not there. My parents allowed me private worlds of my own creation, and they respected them. I imagine they felt the same joy I do when I watch my children playing without me; my daughter opens a bakery as her older brother bounces on a giant rubber ball. The baby fills his garbage truck with blocks. Each of us enters his or her own separate sphere. This, I've realized, is my favorite part of mothering. My looking away and then observing.

When my kids and I stop doing our own things and come together, it's because we want to. The activities we do together offer all of us pleasure; we opt in and because of this, we actually have fun. I may not play, but I'm funny and affectionate, and I love to talk about feelings. I love to teach too: how to count, how to read. It feels good to be with my kids in these specific ways, and to let myself be there. It took some time, but I've realized I can't be every kind of mother. I can only be one. I can only be theirs.

1. The word "unhooked" (Line 3, Para. 1) is closest in meaning to _____.
   A) moved away   B) discovered   C) broke away   D) emulated
2. The author believes that when children play, parents should _____.
   A) stand by   B) try to mediate   C) play with them   D) learn to compromise
3. What's the author's attitude towards her parents' company?
   A) Favorable.   B) Objective.   C) Skeptical.   D) Critical.
4. What does the author argue in the last paragraph?
   A) As parents we should teach less and participate more.
   B) The parent-child interaction should be pleasant for both sides.
   C) Mothers of more than two children have no energy to take part in games.
   D) Parents must explore ways of education suitable for society.
5. Which of the following would be the best title for the text?
   A) Happy Parent-child Time   B) Effective Parental Interference
   C) You Can Be Every Kind of Mom   D) Moms Don't Play

(Text 67)

Attitudes to strangers tend to follow a familiar pattern. Children are taught never to speak to unknown grown-ups, especially those regarded by their parents as untrustworthy. The onset of adolescence and young adulthood brings a bursting desire to interact with all sorts of people, particularly the kind who might not elicit family approval.

Social circles generally narrow again as people find life-partners, form households and produce offspring of their own. Time becomes scarce; new friendships are often based on sharing the burden of child care. Some people never recover the youthful zest for romance. Professional duties swell even as parental ones diminish, and the inclination sags.

But that is not the whole story. In mid-life and beyond people can still experience the joy of a random meeting, however short, which somehow touches a nerve. A sense of mutual understanding that is life-affirming even if the one you met will be never seen again. The knowledge that the exchange will be a one-off can permit a delicious, uninhibited frankness.

In the age of COVID-19 and Zoom, the chronological pattern has become strange. Instead of their hazy possibilities and risks, strangers have assumed an all-too-literal role as a looming source of infection. During lockdowns they are officially to be avoided. Yet many still long for the delight of communion.

Will Buckingham has written a moving memoir of finding solace, after the death of his life-partner, in travelling and talking in lands such as Myanmar that are culturally distant from his native England. The author makes sweeping generalisations about the evolution of human society, from hunter-gatherers to the age of Homer and beyond. He makes two separate but related points. First, interacting meaningfully with a new person can bring huge rewards—but it is a skill that must be cultivated and can easily be lost. Second, the self-segregation of modern Western societies means that, for many people, conversing with some fellow citizens seems pointless, undesirable or eccentric. The second problem makes the first worse: if you consider others beyond the pale, why make the effort to get to know them?

In Britain and America political divisions have turned into tribal ones. Supporters and opponents of Brexit live in separate clusters; Republicans and Democrats see each other as bad people, not fellow Americans whose opinions happen to differ. These opposing sides have become strangers to one another. Mr. Buckingham focuses on the pleasures of encounters in remote places where the stakes are lower because the acquaintanceships are bound to be temporary. But he notes that alertness of unfamiliar people is neither new nor unable to overcome.

1. According to the text, people's attitude towards strangers _____.
   A) changes with age
   B) is related to curiosity
   C) affects family relations
   D) follows the same pattern

2. It is said that when people are middle-aged or older, they _____.
   A) have expanded their circle of friends
   B) have no interest in romances
   C) enjoy random meetings with strangers
   D) cannot be honest with acquaintances

3. Communication in an encounter is more frank because both parties _____.
   A) expect no meeting again
   B) think it novel and feel excited
   C) take a positive attitude
   D) like to tell a whole story

4. In his memoir, Will Buckingham _____.
   A) brings out two contradictory questions
   B) tells about the fun of random meeting
   C) analyzes the evolution of human society
   D) explains cultural traits of varied nations

5. According to the last paragraph, Mr. Buckingham believes that _____.
   A) disputes over interests often keep people alert to strangers
   B) communications in remote places can hardly last long

C) people from different tribes cannot communicate frankly

D) the alertness of unfamiliar people can be overcomed

(Text 68)

The notion that the modern economy lacks "good jobs" is as uncontroversial as saying that Lionel Messi is good at football. Pundits strongly criticize the disappearance of the steady positions of the past, where people did a fair day's work for a fair day's pay. But what if the whole debate rests on shaky foundations?

It certainly lacks historical awareness. Compare the current discussion with the one during America's postwar boom. Few people back then believed that they were living in a golden age of labour. Commentators were instead full of anxiety, worrying about the "blue-collar blues".

In fact the notion that the world of work is in decay is as old as capitalism itself. John Stuart Mill worried in the mid-19th century that the rise of capitalism would provoke social decay. People would focus on nothing other than earning money, he feared, turning them into stupid people with no imagination. The rise of big business and white-collar work in America provoked a new set of anxieties. It was soon predicted that the self-made men of yore would be replaced by weak company drones who did what they were told.

By any reasonable standard work is better today than it was. Pay is higher, working hours are shorter and industrial accidents rarer. 90% of American employees said in 2020 that they were completely or somewhat satisfied with their job security, up from 79% in 1993.

If the jobs-are-bad narrative falls down on the facts, why is it so pervasive—and so intuitive? Partly it is because no one has bothered to look at the evidence. Other observers just don't like the constant change and turbulence which has always been part and parcel of capitalism. Yet perhaps the most important reason is that people dislike acknowledging trade-offs. Mill seemed unable to square his concern about the effects of capitalism with his argument that the division of labour had massively increased living standards.

People often make similar errors today. The decline of trade unions may have hurt some workers' wages; but it is less commonly acknowledged that this has also made it easier for less "traditional" workers to enter the labour market. Sedentary office jobs can make people fat; but people are far less likely to die on the job than they once were.

A relentless focus on the problems of labour markets still has its uses. It encourages people to think about how to make improvements. Today's world of work is far better than its critics would like to admit, but there is every reason to try to make it better still.

1. Lionel Messi is mentioned in the first paragraph to present _____.

A) a related theme

B) a famous saying

C) an analogical case

D) a background story

2. Which of the following statements would John Stuart Mill most likely agree with?

   A) Staff of big businesses could only do what they were told.

   B) People lose creativity because of their passion for money.

   C) The view that the workplace was in decay was out of date.

   D) It's hard to really enhance life standards due to capitalism.

3. The author notes that people can't evaluate the workplace correctly because they _____.

   A) miss the golden age of labour   B) fail to weigh the pros and cons

   C) expect the trade unions to revive   D) dislike the sedentary office jobs

4. What does the author think of the labor market today?

   A) Fairly good.   B) Quite terrible.

   C) Indescribable.   D) Disappointing.

5. Which of the following questions does the author try to answer?

   A) When did the workplace decline the most rapidly?

   B) What changes have taken place in the labor market?

   C) How can we correctly understand views of social critics?

   D) Why are people always gloomy about the world of work?

(Text 69)

As a related study describes, Twitter has come to play a crucial role in the way that news functions during events like the Egyptian revolution—like an overloaded newswire filled with everything from breaking news to rumor and everything in between.

The evolution of what media theorist Jeff Jarvis and others have called "networked journalism" has made the business of news much more chaotic, since it now consists of thousands of voices instead of just a few prominent ones who happen to have the tools to make themselves heard. If there is a growth area in media, it is in the field of "curated news," where real-time filters verify and redistribute the news that comes in from tens of thousands of sources, and use tools like Storify to present a coherent picture of what is happening on the ground.

One of the additional points the study makes is that the personal Twitter accounts belonging to journalists were far more likely to be retweeted or engaged with by others than official accounts for the media outlets they worked for. The point here is one we have tried to make repeatedly: Social media are called social for a reason. They're about human beings connecting with other human beings around an event, and the more that media outlets try to stifle the human aspect of these tools—through repressive social-media policies, for example—the less likely they will be to benefit from using them.

Another benefit of a distributed or networked version of journalism is one sociologist Zeynep Tufekci has made in the course of her research into how Twitter and other social tools affected the events in Tunisia, Egypt, and elsewhere. As she wrote in a recent blog post, one of the realities of mainstream media is what is often called "pack journalism": the kind that sees hundreds of journalists show up for official briefings by government or military sources, but few pursue their own stories outside the official sphere. Tufekci says social media and "citizen journalism" can be a powerful antidote to this kind of process, and that's fundamentally a positive force for journalism.

As we look at the way news and information flows in this new world of social networks, and what Andy Carvin has called "random acts of journalism" by those who may not even see themselves as journalists, it's easy to get distracted by how chaotic the process seems, and how difficult it is to separate the signal from the noise. But more information is better—even if it requires new skills on the part of journalists when it comes to filtering that information—and journalism, as Jay Rosen has pointed out, tends to get better when more people do it.

1. It can be inferred from the first paragraph that _____.
   A) the Egyptian revolution resulted from the application of Twitter
   B) the world financial crises led to the Egyptian revolution
   C) the Egyptian revolution brought Twitter into wide application
   D) Twitter has played a key role in news media during the Egyptian revolution
2. Which of the following is true according to Paragraph 2?
   A) "Networked journalism" has got the business of news into great disorder.
   B) "Networked journalism" is the mainstream of the news media.
   C) "Networked journalism" is dominated by famous people.
   D) The business of news will develop quickly due to Twitter.
3. The word "retweeted" (Line 2, Para. 3) probably means _____.
   A) retreated   B) hailed   C) sent   D) forwarded
4. By saying "pack journalism"(Line 4, Para. 4), the author probably means _____.
   A) news will be packed like a baggage
   B) "citizen journalism" will replace "networked journalism"
   C) the journalists prefer "networked journalism"
   D) the journalists depend on official briefings, so homogeneous news reporting emerges
5. What is the text centered on?
   A) Twitter is getting more and more important in modern journalism.
   B) How journalism works in the age of Twitter.
   C) Networked journalism is superior to the traditional journalism.
   D) More and more people prefer Twitter.

(Text 70)

The intense desire of international families to send their children to college in the United States is a major factor driving demand for improved education in many foreign markets. But enrollment in U.S. higher education institutions among those students has shown recent signs of "flattening," a new report concludes.

Overall, the number of international students studying in the United States rose by 3.4 percent, to 1.078 million students, during the 2016–17 school year. Nearly 35,000 more students enrolled in U.S. institutions during that period on non-immigrant student visas, according to the *Open Doors* report, published annually by the nonprofit Institute of International Education (IIE). It's the 11th straight year that the *Open Doors* report has recorded growth in the number of international students in U.S. colleges and universities. But at the same time, the number of new international students—those who were enrolled at a U.S. institution for the first time in the fall of 2016—fell for the first time in 12 years since *Open Doors* began reporting that piece of data.

There's an explanation for the disconnection between the overall, rising enrollment of foreign students and the drop-off in new enrollees:

Even though fewer new foreign students started this year at U.S. colleges, there was a relatively large pool of other students already taking part in degree programs and choosing to stay for additional training, said Sharon Witherell, a spokeswoman for the institute. In other words, a large number of students were already on U.S. campuses and working their way through programs—and fewer of those students left than in previous years. And while the drop in new international students is small as a piece of the overall population, it could be signaling the start of a larger decline, Witherell said.

The IIE conducted an additional online survey of 500 U.S. higher education institutions, which found that they reported an average 7 percent decline in new students. If that is correct and the trend continues, it may not be long before U.S. institutions start to see an overall drop in the number of foreign students, she said. Officials with the institute cited a number of "global and local economic conditions" for tamping down the number of new students coming from abroad.

One factor is a scaling down of large government scholarship programs in Saudi Arabia and Brazil. Most of those nations have been big contributors of students coming to the United States. Another contributor to the weak numbers of new enrollees is that more students are seeking "optional practical training" focused on their academic fields after obtaining degrees in the United States. That means those students are staying longer in the U.S. higher education system.

1. The word "flattening" (Line 3, Para. 1) is closest in meaning to _____.
   A) levelling off　　　　　　　　　　　　B) cutting down
   C) rising and falling　　　　　　　　　　D) being vague
2. We can infer from the finding of *Open Doors* report that _____.
   A) more overseas families plan to send their children to U.S. institutes
   B) the number of international students in the U.S. has slowly been going down
   C) the number of U.S. overseas students is 3.4% higher than that of 11 years ago
   D) foreign students in the U.S. kept on increasing in the past decade or so
3. Sharon Witherell predicted that _____.
   A) more foreign students were enrolled in U.S. institutes
   B) more students would choose to stay for more training

C) the number of new students may keep on dropping

D) new comers on U.S. campuses were sharply decreasing

4. Saudi Arabia and Brazil were mentioned as the example of _____.

A) the main source countries of overseas students in the U.S.

B) countries with the highest subsidies for studying abroad

C) countries opposed to studying in the United States

D) typical countries eager to send more overseas students

5. Which of the following would be the best title for the text?

A) A Major Factor Driving the Demand for Improved Overseas Education

B) Number of Foreign College Students in the U.S. Shows Signs of "Flattening"

C) The United States: Still the Main Destination of Overseas Study

D) Why Are There Fewer Overseas Students in the U.S. Colleges?

(Text 71)

The human brain is born to map our surroundings. This trait is called spatial memory—our ability to remember certain locations and where objects are in relation to one another. New findings published today in *Scientific Reports* suggest that one major feature of our spatial recall is efficiently locating high-calorie, energy-rich food. The study's authors believe human spatial memory ensured that our hunter-gatherer ancestors could prioritize the location of reliable nutrition, giving them an evolutionary leg up.

In a taste test, the 512 participants of the study were nearly 30 percent more accurate at mapping the high-calorie samples versus the low-calorie ones, regardless of how much they liked those foods or odors. They were also 243 percent more accurate when presented with actual foods, as opposed to the food scents.

"Our main takeaway message is that human minds seem to be designed for efficiently locating high-calorie foods in our environment," says Rachelle de Vries, a Ph.D. candidate in human nutrition and health at Wageningen University and lead author of the new paper. "Those with a better memory for where and when high-calorie food resources would be available were likely to have a survival—or fitness—advantage," she explains.

We tend to think of primates such as ourselves as having lost the acute sense of smell seen in many other mammals in favor of sharp eyesight. And to a large degree, we humans have developed that way. But the new findings support the notion that our nose is not altogether terrible: "These results suggest that human minds continue to house a cognitive system optimized for energy—efficient food-hunting within erratic food habitats of the past, and highlight the often underestimated capabilities of the human smelling sense," the authors wrote.

One drawback of our spatial skills, as they relate to sustenance, is our modern taste for junk food. Chronic diseases such as diabetes were not a concern for our ancestors. If you came across a rich grove of fruit trees, you consumed all the sugar you could to help ensure your survival. Now our taste for sweets and fats contributes to a global obesity epidemic and has us reaching for candy over lettuce. "In a way, our minds and bodies may be mismatched to our current food-rich circumstances," de Vries says.

"We're more likely to remember sweet things, which was a real plus for most of our evolutionary history," adds James Nairne, a cognitive psychology professor at Purdue University. "But this is problematic in today's world… We're still walking around with Stone Age brains."

1. At the beginning of the text, the author introduces the topic by _____.
   A) raising a question   B) defining a concept
   C) describing a phenomenon   D) offering a proposal
2. Which of the following statements would de Vries most probably agree with?
   A) Human spatial memory is related with survival.
   B) High calorie foods give off more noticeable odors.
   C) High calorie foods can shorten life expectancy.
   D) Having sweets is essential to human survival.
3. About human sense of smell, which of the following is true?
   A) It's worse than that of other mammals.   B) It degenerated with the evolution of vision.
   C) It's mainly used to assist in food-hunting. D) It's better than we previously imagined.
4. What does Nairne mean by saying "We're still walking around with Stone Age brains"?
   A) Our brains are as good as they were in the Stone Age.
   B) Our brains are only adapted to Stone Age environments.
   C) Our spatial memory retains the traits of the Stone Age.
   D) Our brains are still influenced by Stone Age memories.
5. Which of the following would be the best title for the text?
   A) Why Do We Like Sweet Food?   B) Human Brain, Still a Calorie Hunter
   C) The Evolution of Our Sense of Smell   D) Spatial Memory and Fast Food

Text 72

The British exam system has been plunged into fresh disarray by COVID-19 but the debate over grade inflation, the credibility of exam qualifications and the dangers of fact-cramming have been going on in this country, without pause, for 164 years. The first formal school examinations in the UK took place in the late 1850s, part of a reforming drive to standardise entry to universities. Those exams went on for a week, with separate papers morning, afternoon and evening. They included papers on English language and literature, history, geography, geology, Greek, Latin, French, German, physical sciences, political economy, law, zoology, mathematics, chemistry, arithmetic, drawing, music and religious knowledge. They were extremely difficult.

For any parent who thinks their A-levels were harder than those sat by their children, here is a sample of what their forebears struggled with in the first senior examination for 17-year-olds in 1858: Obtain the sum of forty-six times seven thousand and twenty, seventeen times one million and one, and thirty-three times thirty-three.

The University of Oxford set up a Delegacy of Local Examinations in 1857, and the following year Cambridge University held the first public examinations for 370 pupils in various cities, including Bristol, Birmingham and London. Dons in full academic dress administered the exams, travelling around the country by train carrying the exam papers in locked boxes.

But while there was general agreement on the answers to these initial tests, there was no consensus on whether they actually measured intelligence or aptitude for scholarship. The first Cambridge examiners complained that students had absorbed multiple facts before sitting exams but with little understanding: "Their answers, even when accurate, showed a general uniformity of expression which seemed to imply that poor handbooks had been placed before the students to be 'got up' and that little attempt had been made by their instructors to excite the interest of their pupils by questionings or remarks of their own."

Then, as now, exam results became an obsession. The Board of Education, established at the end of Victoria's reign, noted that "examinations as ends in themselves have occupied too much the thoughts of parents and teachers". Others complained that by focusing on "correct" answers in a specified range of subjects, the experience of education was being narrowed. In 1926 the National Union of Teachers warned that "the compulsory system of examination would drive joy out of the schools".

1. According to Paragraph 1, what can we learn about the British exam system?
   A) It has been affected negatively by the high inflation during the COVID-19 epidemic.
   B) The examiners have lost credibility to promote fact-cramming.
   C) The first tests were put in place to standardise entry to universities.
   D) COVID-19 helps to settle down the dispute about the exam system.

2. The sample in the first senior examination in 1858 was used to illustrate _____.
   A) the scope of the test   B) the difficulty of the test
   C) the struggle parents experienced   D) the long time the test took

3. One criticism of the British examination system is that _____.
   A) it fails to predict academic performance
   B) it encourages fact-cramming without comprehension
   C) students' answers in tests are different
   D) it's harder for teachers to impart knowledge

4. The overall attitude towards the system of examinations is _____.
   A) negative   B) neutral   C) affirmative   D) puzzled

5. Which of the following might be the best title for this text?
   A) Prestigious Universities Led the Examination System
   B) Rows over Exams Have Raged for over 160 years
   C) Difficulty of Tests Declines with Time
   D) Examinations Drive Joy out of the Schools

Text 73

How do you do long division? What are prime numbers? How do verbs work? And where exactly is Australia? These are just some of the questions that parents have been looking up online, as home schooling has forced mothers and fathers to rediscover long-forgotten lessons.

Analysis of Google search trends found thousands of extra queries for working out percentages, using semi-colons, and the number of bones in the body. Topics including geography, science, maths and English had dramatic rises, with parents looking for tips for their children's worksheets. Core subjects top the table for parents wondering how to help their children, according to the research by the shoe manufacturer Clarks.

The monthly number of searches for "what is a factor in maths" rose by nearly 2,500 per cent compared with April 2019. "What is a mean", "what are prime numbers" and "how to work out percentages" also showed increases. Adjectives, adverbs, nouns, pronouns and prepositions also prompted a lot of desperate googling. However, verbs tripped parents up the most, with 334 per cent more attempts to understand them using the search engine.

The counties of the UK, the countries of Africa and Asia, and exactly where Australia have also been a source of confusion, the data suggests. Rosie McKissock, a manager at Clarks, said: "As a parent myself, I totally recognise what this survey describes. It's been a humbling experience taking on home schooling for two young children, realising the patience involved in teaching kids as well as the revelation of just how much you have forgotten, or perhaps never knew in the first place."

Parent Ping, a daily survey app, found that 40 per cent of parents said this lockdown was harder than the first. Private tutoring services have experienced a rise in demand, with some parents willing to pay up to £1,500 a week. A survey of parents found more than half had resorted to Google to help their children with home schooling. More parents relied on the search engine than turned to other educational resources such as BBC Bitesize, or even contacting teachers.

Maths was the hardest to teach—as reported by more than half of parents. The least popular subject for home schooling was IT.

1. Long division and prime numbers are mentioned to show that _____.

    A) there should be qualifications for parents

    B) they are important to rediscover lessons

    C) they are easy to solve

    D) parents have multiple questions when teaching children at home

2. It can be learned from Paragraph 2 that _____.

    A) thousands of parents are interested in working out percentages

    B) parents resort to the Internet to aid their children's study

    C) only core subjects deserve parents' attention

    D) extensive studies about maths are available online

3. What does the phrase "trip...up" (Line 4, Para. 3) most probably mean?

    A) Cause sb. to cry.   B) Walk lightly.

    C) Detect a fault.   D) Perplex sb.

4. McKissock recognises taking on home schooling as a humbling experience because _____.

    A) only modest parents are qualified for home schooling

    B) teaching two children at the same time causes confusion

    C) it requires patience and enough knowledge for parents

    D) teaching is even out of reach for successful managers

5. The search trends of parents can be partly ascribed to _____.

    A) the impact of COVID-19 pandemic   B) the high expense of private tuition

    C) the unreliability of educational resources   D) the popularity of IT in home schooling

(Text 74)

It is the holy grail of parenthood: a scientific consensus on the perfect bedtime routine for those young children who discover an irrepressible lust for life just at the moment when daylight wanes and duvets beckon. A Medical Research Council-funded study into the only roadmap that really matters to parents of children aged two to eight has identified six key goals and a scoring system that—when bedtime descends, yet again, into anarchy—flags the phases that parents are missing.

Dr. George Kitsaras, a psychologist at the University of Manchester who led the study, said: "Bedtime routines are important family activities and have important implications on children's well-being, development and health. But up to now there has been no real scientific consensus. We need to untie the conflicting signals and messages that parents receive." He added, "This lack of a clear consensus-based definition has limited health professionals' ability to communicate best practice effectively with families. This study provides that expert and scientific guidance for the first time."

Children's bedtime can be one of the most stressful times of the day for parents. The tensions that start shortly after birth, and memorably narrated by Samuel Jackson—are championed on the one side by the "baby trainers", who feel it is essential to let babies learn to cry themselves to sleep, and on the other side by "natural parents", who believe every cry should be soothed.

As children age, experts' opinions rely on the research that shows the bad impact sleeplessness has on a child's physical, mental and academic well-being. Recent US research suggests children with inconsistent sleep schedules have higher body mass index percentiles, and experts and sleep charities have said the coronavirus crisis is disrupting sleep patterns even further by heightening children's anxiety and disturbing previously established routines.

Kitsaras's study, Defining and Measuring Bedtime Routines in Families with Young Children, devises two different ways of scoring bedtime routines: one that measures a single routine, and another that collates activity over seven days.

All activities around bedtime matter for children's development and well-being. But from the wide range of activities around bedtime, tooth brushing is considered to be the most important to remember each night. "There are strong links between inadequate oral hygiene practices and dental decay in children and adults." he said. For children, early childhood caries can lead to higher occurrence of dental disease in later life and, in some cases, untreated childhood caries can lead to extractions. Washing or having a shower each night before bed, on the other hand, might be a common practice for families but the experts considered it to be part of a wider umbrella of child-parent interactions rather than an independent practice we need to specifically target.

1. The phrase "holy grail" (Line 1, Para. 1) is closest in meaning to _____.
   A) dream   B) distress   C) pressure   D) responsibility

2. According to Dr. George Kitsaras, children's bedtime _____.
   A) tends to descend into anarchy   B) becomes a headache for parents
   C) needs consistent expert guidance   D) reflects the development of children

3. The author mentions the narration by Samuel Jackson to illustrate _____.
   A) the causes of bedtime anxiety   B) the great pressure upon parents
   C) the expert opinions on children's growth   D) the contradictory theories about bedtime

4. Why is tooth brushing considered to be the most important bedtime routine?
   A) Because it tends to be ignored by parents.
   B) Because it has a long-term impact on dental health.
   C) Because it is a part of child-parent interactions.
   D) Because it matters in adults' life.

5. Which of the following can be inferred about Kitsaras's study?
   A) It focuses on the effects of sleeplessness on a child's well-being.
   B) It provides consistent and operable expert guidance on children's bedtime.
   C) It highlights the importance of bedtime routines for the first time.
   D) It overthrows the theories of "baby trainers" and "natural parents".

(Text 75)

Science fiction writers have been dreaming of a crewed mission to Mars for over a century. But it wasn't until Wernher von Braun published the English translation of his book, *The Mars Project*, in 1953 that the idea was plucked out of the realm of fiction and into reality. *The Mars Project* makes an impressive case for the technical feasibility of getting to Mars, outlining with extraordinary specificity how 10 space vehicles, each manned with 70 people and using conventional propellant, could achieve a round-trip voyage to the Red Planet.

Although science has developed considerably since the book was published, challenges still remain, from designing a breathable habitat to growing nutritious food. But there's another issue that a NASA research project called the Center for the Utilization of Biological Engineering in Space (CUBES) has been working on since 2017, one that is as essential to the long-term success of an off-planet human settlement as air or food: treating illness.

It's a tricky problem that doesn't have an easy answer. What about packing the shuttle full of medicine? This might seem like a realistic solution at first glance, but astronauts can't know in advance all of the ways they could get sick. There are some known risks to sending human life to Mars, such as the effects of the planet's lower gravity on bone density and muscle mass or potential exposure to cosmic radiation as astronauts leave the protective cover of Earth's atmosphere. But packing medicines for every contingency would be expensive and take up precious cargo space.

Nor could astronauts depend on timely shipments from Earth, due to the long distance between our planet and Mars. The spacecraft that have landed on Mars have taken the better part of a year to get there. Perseverance, the most recent robotic rover sent to Mars on July 30, 2020, is expected to land by the time you read this: more than 200 days after launch. That's far too long to deliver urgent, lifesaving medications or supplies.

Rather than sending astronauts into space with a costly and finite stock of medicines, scientists have approached the problem a little differently. What if astronauts could manufacture on Mars what they need? This is one of the solutions that CUBES, a Space Technology Research Institute established by NASA in February 2017, is attempting to develop. And it is doing so using the tools and techniques of synthetic biology—a scientific field that uses engineering to build new biological organisms on demand.

1. *The Mars Project* is mentioned to illustrate _____.

    A) the best-seller of science fictions   B) a case for the feasibility of getting to Mars

    C) the power of conventional propellant   D) the best work of Wernher von Braun

2. CUBES is endeavouring to address the problem of _____.

    A) creating habitable space settlements

    B) cultivating nutritious crops in outer space

    C) supplying the indispensable oxygen to astronauts

    D) treating illnesses of astronauts

3. It can be learned that one health problem for astronauts is caused by _____.

    A) inadequate medicine supply in the space shuttle

    B) cramped space where they work and live

    C) lack of shield from Earth's atmosphere

    D) unaffordability of effective medications

4. The author's attitude toward shipping medicines from Earth is _____.

    A) negative   B) uncertain   C) positive   D) tentative

5. Which of the following might be the best title for the text?

    A) The Invincible Red Planet   B) Medicine for Mars

    C) Turning Fiction into Reality   D) The Latest Mars Rover

(Text 76)

The early history of the alphabet may require rewriting. Four clay artefacts found at an ancient site in Syria have what is potentially the earliest alphabetic writing ever found. The discovery suggests that the alphabet emerged 500 years earlier than we thought.

A popular idea is that the alphabet first appeared in Egypt some 3,800 years ago, when about 20 Egyptian hieroglyphs were repurposed as the first alphabet's letters. But a discovery at the roughly 4,300-year-old site of Umm el-Marra in Syria challenges this. During excavations in 2004, Glenn Schwartz at Johns Hopkins University and his colleagues found four lumps of clay the size and shape of human fingers, each inscribed with between one and five symbols.

"When I first saw them, I thought: this looks like writing," says Schwartz, but it was clearly unlike the ancient writing form typical of the time and place. After considering other possibilities— for instance, that the symbols were from script used by the Indus civilisation—Schwartz now argues that these may be early alphabetic letters. He thinks versions of the letters A, L, O and K are present, although it isn't clear what words they might spell out.

If the clay fingers are as old as claimed, they would "<u>blow</u> our current theories about the invention of the alphabet <u>clear out of the water</u>", says Aaron Koller at Yeshiva University, New York. Koller wonders if Schwartz somehow misdated the artefacts—although Schwartz is sure he didn't.

Benjamin Sass at Tel Aviv University, Israel, says the Umm el-Marra symbols, whatever they are, don't look like early alphabetic signs to him, so they don't pose a challenge to existing ideas of the alphabet's invention. But John Darnell at Yale University is more open to the idea that the alphabet is older than we thought. "All writing has a proto-history no doubt, so the signs Schwartz has published could really represent such a thing," he says.

There is some evidence that there was trade between Egypt and the ancient cities of what is now northern Syria, says Schwartz, so it is still conceivable the alphabet emerged in Egypt and was then carried north to Umm el-Marra. Whatever the sequence of events, the consensus is that the alphabet wasn't the official writing system of any political state much before about 3,200 years ago. This suggests it was passed down through many generations as an informal script that wasn't used by royals or the powerful elite.

1. What is true about the artefacts found in Syria?

   A) They challenge the existing idea of the alphabet's invention.

   B) They are 500 years older than people previously thought.

   C) They are the earliest artefacts discovered by archaeologists.

   D) They suggest that the alphabet has changed greatly with time.

2. Schwartz believes the symbols on the clay fingers _____.

   A) do not look like writing   B) can be grouped into many words

   C) were the early forms of several letters   D) were adapted from the Indus script

3. What does the phrase "blow...clear out of the water" (Lines 1~2, Para. 4) most probably mean?

    A) Overturn something completely.   B) Overstate or exaggerate greatly.

    C) Dilute the value of something.   D) Prove something is reasonable.

4. John Darnell is more open to the idea of older alphabet by pointing out that _____ .

    A) existing theories are proposed based on speculation

    B) scientific hypotheses should be open to new ideas

    C) the proto-history began much earlier than we thought

    D) the symbols may be the predecessors of alphabetic letters

5. According to Schwartz, it was possible that trade played an important role in _____ .

    A) developing the alphabet into a writing system in Egypt

    B) spreading the alphabet to Umm el-Marra

    C) passing down the alphabet from generation to generation

    D) ending the monopoly of those in power on the alphabet

(Text 77)

TikTok is the most famous example of a Chinese social media app that became very popular overseas, but in the Middle East there is a second Chinese-founded app that is taking the region by storm. Yalla, or "Let's go" in Arabic, saw the monthly users of its chat app and its games app rise nearly fivefold to more than 12m in the year to last June.

The company has localised so well, with headquarters in Dubai, that many users are unaware that its engineering team and founders are all in Hangzhou, near Shanghai—a rare example of a successful Chinese-foreign hybrid tech company.

Yang Tao, the company's chief executive, spent the first six years of his career in Abu Dhabi working for telecoms equipment firm ZTE, which is how he met his co-founders, as well as group president Saifi Ismail, the most senior Arab manager who is also on the board. Mr. Yang said he came up with the idea while travelling in the region, from Egypt to Afghanistan, and noticing how much time people spent talking on the phone. He decided to build a social network based around chatting, rather than typing, and today each user spends an average of five hours in the app, much of it not actively talking, but hanging out or listening, akin to having a radio on in the background.

When he started, there was little interest. But he said that it was much easier to grow an app in the Middle East than in his home market. He took inspiration from China's live streaming platforms, where millions of users tune in to watch their favourite stars, but then decided to create an app that would enable people to socialise in small groups. Unlike Clubhouse, a more recent voice-based social network, Yalla is mostly centred on small rooms of up to 20 people, who are invited in by their friends. Mr. Yang described the idea as a virtual gathering—describing the social gatherings he used to attend in Abu Dhabi. And, like a gathering, guests bring gifts: Yalla's profits come from the in-app virtual presents that users send to one another.

Yalla's offices in Hangzhou are filled with 350 staff, including graphics designers who animate the in-app gifts, front-end developers for the app interface, and teams developing new apps, such as its recently launched Yalla Ludo multiplayer game, which now contributes the majority of its revenues. The company saw huge growth during last year's COVID lockdowns, and Mr. Yang said the apps had momentum after being recommended on Apple and Google's regional app store homepages for several months.

1. Which of the following is true about Yalla?

   A) It is second only to TikTok in terms of popularity around the world.

   B) It experienced a rise of 12 million users in a period of one year.

   C) It is quite popular in the Middle East.

   D) It has more users of its chap app than its games app.

2. ZTE is mentioned in Paragraph 3 to show _____.

   A) how successful Chinese telecom companies are

   B) how experienced the company's founders are

   C) how the target market of Yalla was chosen

   D) how Yang Tao met his partners to launch the app

3. Nowadays, users use Yalla _____.

   A) by hanging out or listening

   B) to connect with famous stars

   C) as a substitute for live broadcasts on radio

   D) to reduce expenditure spent on the phone

4. Yalla makes money by _____.

   A) attracting venture investors

   B) issuing virtual gifts that users send to one another

   C) raising money through gatherings

   D) charging for the traffic of chat rooms

5. According to Yang Tao, when did the apps have momentum?

   A) When Yalla was founded in Shanghai.

   B) After they had been recommended by Apple and Google.

   C) Before COVID Lockdowns.

   D) During his six years of career in Abu Dhabi.

(Text 78)

Bosworth, the head of Facebook's augmented- and virtual-reality research labs, had just shared a blog post outlining his group's vision for the future of human-computer interaction. Then he tweeted a photo of a wearable—something that looks like an iPod Mini mounted on a thick wristband.

This device translates motor nerve signals into digital commands. To put it plainly, it's a new way for humans to control computers. When it's on, you can just flick your fingers in space to manipulate virtual inputs, whether you're using a VR headset or interacting with the real world. You can also "train" it to sense the intention of your fingers, so that actions happen even when your fingers are at rest. The nameless device is just a concept, and Bosworth says the technology could become widely available in five to 10 years.

In a virtual demonstration, a person was shown wearing the wrist device and playing a video game without moving their fingers. These kinds of demos tend to gesture toward mind-reading tech, but Bosworth insists it is not that. Here, he says, the wearer's mind is creating signals identical to those that make the thumb move, without moving the thumb. The device records an intention to move the thumb. "We don't know what's happening in the brain," he says, "until someone sends a signal down the wire."

Bosworth also emphasizes that the wearable is different from the invasive implants used in a 2019 brain-computer interface study that Facebook was involved in or Elon Musk's Neuralink tech.

In other words, Facebook isn't reading our minds, even if it already knows a lot about what's going on in our heads.

There's a question of why Facebook—largely a software company—wants to own this new computing paradigm. And why we should trust it. "Sometimes these companies have cash piles large enough to invest in these huge R&D projects, and they'll take a loss if it means they can be front-runners in the future," says Michelle Richardson, director of the Data and Privacy Project at the nonprofit Center for Democracy and Technology. But, she notes, it's difficult to overhaul products once they're built—which is why it's important to start conversations about privacy and other implications early in the process.

Bosworth says Facebook sees tech like this as fundamental to connecting people. If anything, the past year has shown us the importance of connecting, he says. He also seems to believe he can earn the required trust by not "surprising" customers: "You say what you do, you set expectations, and you deliver on those expectations over time. Trust arrives on foot and leaves on horseback."

1. What do we know about the new wearable device?

   A) It enables a user to interact with the computer.

   B) It interprets the signals sent by computers.

   C) It functions like an iPod Mini on a wristband.

   D) It senses only the obvious movements of fingers.

2. Bosworth insists the new device differs from mind-reading tech in that _____.

   A) it doesn't understand the intention to move fingers

   B) it can receive signals directly from the brain

   C) it allows one to interpret gestures when he plays games

   D) it depends on the signals sent from a computer

3. Neuralink tech is mentioned in Paragraph 4 to present _____.

   A) a cause analysis   B) a supporting theory

   C) a contrasting example   D) background knowledge

4. Which of the following statements would Michelle Richardson most probably agree with?

   A) Companies with much more capital are keener on risk investment.

   B) Possible problems brought by the new tech should be discussed early.

   C) Software companies cannot be allowed to study computing models.

   D) Conversations about privacy and other implications are not necessary.

5. Bosworth's attitude towards winning users' trust is _____.

   A) contradictory   B) ambiguous   C) unmindful   D) confident

Text 79

Cyndi Williams, a chemical engineer by training and a one-time software engineer by trade, never meant to get into healthcare. But in 2014, an unexpected conversation with a colleague at global software consultancy ThoughtWorks changed her trajectory.

During one of their bi-weekly mentoring sessions, Isabella Degen revealed that she was one of the 400,000 people across the UK living with Type 1 Diabetes, a disease that required her to inject insulin multiple times a day, working from crude formulas and personal experience to determine how much to dose and when. She was leaving the company to create an app to make that easier for others in her situation—and she needed help.

Williams' interest was aroused. That year, Williams and Degan founded Quin. The app tracks users' data and makes the careful analysis in the context in order to produce highly personalised recommendations that patients no longer need inject insulin by guessing to regulate insulin levels .

Williams is relying on this super-personalisation model to make Quin surpass its competitors in the booming mobile health market, predicted to be worth $189 billion by 2025. And, so far, the market seems enthusiastic about her approach. Since its launch in 2014, Quin has received £3.6 million in investor funding, and more than 17,000 users have downloaded the iOS app since it was released in the UK and Ireland last October.

Quin, a tool of "quantifying intuition", relies on a combination of predictive algorithms and personal data, which can be collected automatically or added manually. To get started, users input information about their food intake, insulin doses, activity and blood sugar levels over the course of their day. Once the app has enough information about how certain factors affect the user's blood sugar levels, it's able to suggest specific insulin dosage amounts to regulate them, and graph how the user's blood sugar levels are likely to change over the next five hours. Part of the secret to designing an app people actually want to use, Williams explains, is creating the product with them: since 2014, Quin has consulted more than 300 patients as part of their research programme.

As Quin prepares to launch in the US at the end of this summer, the company is looking into measuring and tracking other physical, psychological and behavioural data, such as sleep and stress, to provide more comprehensive recommendations. But where social media and entertainment apps are designed to keep users checking in as much as possible, Williams hopes that, over time, Quin users will feel confident enough in the app's recommendations that they find themselves opening the app less and less.

1. Isabella Degen wanted to found Quin to _____.
   A) realize personalized diagnosis   B) manage data of the patients
   C) seek a technological breakthrough   D) assist the patients like her
2. Cyndi Williams expects Quin to _____.
   A) surpass other competitive mobile health apps
   B) receive positive responses from customers
   C) reach the market value of $189 billion by 2025
   D) attract more investor funds and users
3. According to Paragraph 5, Quin can help its users to _____.
   A) create medical products independently
   B) inject insulin accurately and scientifically
   C) delete unnecessary health information
   D) know factors affecting blood sugar levels

4. Williams expects Quin's customers to _____.

    A) open the app as much as possible   B) trust the recommendations made by the app

    C) reduce dependence on mobile apps   D) abandon irrational decision-making

5. What is this text centered on?

    A) A creative way to analyze medical information.

    B) A changed trajectory of a software engineer.

    C) An app making diabetes more manageable.

    D) An emerging medical company.

(Text 80)

In May 2020, Prodoscore, a California-based productivity software startup, reported that, based on internal data collected from its 30,000 users, remote working during the coronavirus pandemic was making workers more productive. Prodoscore is part of a new wave of productivity tools, informally known as "tattleware", which enable managers to monitor and time-track their employees' activities while working remotely.

Research consultancy firm Gartner estimates that by the end of 2020, 80 per cent of companies will be using monitoring tools to keep tabs on their employees, including their emails, social media messages and biometric data. These apps use these digital traces to create a profile of individual productivity. For instance, project management tool Asana offers the option to calculate an "influence" score for workers based on how many projects they share and invitations they send. The app also includes a feature called Workload, which lets managers see employees' ongoing projects and reassign tasks if they feel a particular employee is overloaded.

Of course, white-collar workers are not the only quantified employees in the workforce. Long-haul truck drivers are monitored with electronic logging devices that keep track of their location and speeds to help them schedule sleeping and driving periods. Professional athletes are constantly monitored with activity sensors that track workload and fatigue.

These new tools are, of course, ripe for misuse when it comes to privacy and security concerns. But when used transparently and legally, they can provide a rich stream of information that allows companies and workers to understand and improve their productivity and engagement.

In 2016, mathematician Duncan Watts initiated a project with Microsoft dubbed the Organizational Spectroscope, with the goal of applying machine learning modelling to data including email metadata, office locations and job titles. Early results showed that it was able to predict employee satisfaction based on email response time and measure work-life balance from the volume of email sent outside of office hours. In research conducted at Facebook in 2018, psychologist Adam Grant found that employees who didn't respond to the company's two annual surveys were 2.6 times more likely to quit in the following six months.

Perhaps the most fascinating series of experiments were conducted at the MIT Human Dynamics Laboratory by researcher Alex Pentland. Using an electronic badge capable of capturing a vast spectrum of behavioural data, like tone of voice and body language, Pentland studied more than

20 teams in settings including hospitals and call centres. The most <u>telltale</u> sign of a productive team was the level of social engagement between employees. More productive teams had more energetic conversations—not just with their leaders, and outside scheduled meetings.

1. We can learn from the first two paragraphs that Prodoscore _____.
   A) enables the employees to share their working data
   B) can remotely monitor the work of the employees
   C) is used to enhance productivity during the pandemic
   D) is going to be used by about 80 percent of companies

2. Drivers and athletes are mentioned in Paragraph 3 to _____.
   A) explain how to quantify people's workload   B) display the wide use of monitoring tools
   C) exemplify the problem of fatigue   D) testify the necessity of keeping tracks

3. When it comes to privacy and security concerns about the new tools, the author thinks that they _____.
   A) can hardly gain full attention   B) may lead to some legal disputes
   C) are caused by immature operation   D) can be avoided by proper use

4. The word "telltale" (Line 4, Para. 6) is closest in meaning to _____.
   A) illustrative   B) legendary   C) traditional   D) warning

5. The author seems to think that tools like Prodoscore _____.
   A) are worth of further study   B) have many limitations
   C) may improve workers' productivity   D) cannot violate privacy

Text 81

Digital collaboration platforms and online privacy and safety tools are two of the most important tech "enablers" schools are counting on, because proper use of these resources can promote equity and bridge learning gaps during crises such as the COVID-19 pandemic, a new report says. The report, published by the Consortium for School Networking, identifies five tech enablers, which it defines as innovations that help schools surmount various hurdles to learning. The report is the second part of the consortium's yearly series on K-12 (education from kindergarten to 12th grade) tech innovation.

COVID-19 has accelerated the use of digital collaboration platforms in various parts of the world. One case of a K-12 collaboration tool cited in the report follows from the work of St. Vincent Ferrer Catholic School in Delray Beach, Fla., which used Zoom and Skype to collaborate with students from the Roosevelt School in Peru in creating a philanthropy program which yielded a $13,500 award from a U.S.-based contest known as Philanthropy Tank. The award supported an elementary school for migrant children, the Hope Rural School in Indiantown, Fla.

Further, educators in places like India are <u>leveraging</u> mobile apps and one-way communications platforms like radio and TV, to support learning during the pandemic, the report states.

Online privacy and safety tools are assisting schools looking to provide innovative learning approaches during the ongoing COVID-19 pandemic, said Laura Geringer, director of CoSN's Driving K-12 Innovation division.

One strategy for improving online safety is through professional development, focused on boosting educators' competence and equipping teachers with tools and strategies for teaching students about privacy protections. The need to protect privacy poses a complex range of issues for schools, who must guard against hacks, data breaches, unauthorized information sharing, cyberbullying, and other threats. Communities of practice and professional organizations can be powerful K-12 allies in addressing privacy and safety issues in education, according to the report.

CoSN leads the Trusted Learning Environment, which provides guidance, community, and a seal to recognize school systems that meet data privacy standards. Further, Child-net International develops policy recommendations and resources for a range of age groups around topics including cyberbullying, and Common Sense Media offers reviews of websites, apps, and other media, sortable by age, CoSN noted.

The report also included five recommendations for strengthening online privacy in schools: They should integrate digital and online privacy and safety across their organization as a regular priority; teach responsible behaviors for digital and online privacy and safety; build trust with vendors, parents, and students; build leadership capacity and a culture prioritizing privacy; and, prioritize equity, access, and accessibility.

1. What can we infer from the first paragraph?

   A) Digital platforms pose new risks to personal privacy.

   B) Online resources can be conducive to education equality.

   C) The COVID-19 pandemic spurs educational innovation.

   D) CoSN's report identifies several obstacles to learning.

2. The word "leveraging" (Line 1, Para. 3) is closest in meaning to _____.

   A) making use of   B) keeping balance of

   C) appealing for   D) making comparison between

3. The author reveals COVID-19's impact on the use of digital platforms by _____.

   A) analyzing causes   B) presenting data

   C) giving examples   D) describing a phenomenon

4. Which is one of the main functions of the Consortium for School Networking?

   A) It helps and guides schools to create a safe e-learning environment.

   B) It is responsible for evaluating different digital collaboration platforms.

   C) It enables the digital platforms to meet the data privacy standards.

   D) It helps to develop policy recommendations for the authorities.

5. What is the text centered on?

   A) Recent advance in K-12 Tech Innovations in the COVID-19 pandemic.

   B) Recommendations for strengthening online privacy.

   C) A report on creating safe digital collaboration platforms for K-12 students.

   D) The leadership of the Consortium for School Networking.

Text 82

Recent research suggests that most languages that have ever existed are no longer spoken. Dozens of these dead languages are also considered to be lost, or "undeciphered"—that is, we don't know enough about their grammar or vocabulary to be able to actually understand their texts. Lost languages are more than a mere academic curiosity; without them, we miss an entire body of knowledge about the people who spoke them.

However, researchers at MIT's Computer Science and Artificial Intelligence Laboratory (CSAIL) recently made a major development in this area: a new system that has been shown to be able to automatically decipher a lost language, without needing advanced knowledge of its relation to other languages. They also showed that their system can itself determine relationships between languages, and they used it to prove recent scholarship suggesting that the language of Iberian is not actually related to Basque. The team's ultimate goal is for the system to be able to decipher lost languages that have puzzled linguists for decades, using just a few thousand words.

Led by MIT Professor Regina Barzilay, the system relies on several principles grounded in insights from historical linguistics, such as the fact that languages generally only evolve in certain predictable ways. The researchers developed a decipherment algorithm, which can segment words in an ancient language and map them to counterparts in a related language.

With the new system, the relationship between languages is inferred by the algorithm. This question is one of the biggest challenges in decipherment. For Iberian, the scholars still cannot agree on the related language: Some argue for Basque, while others refute this hypothesis and claim that Iberian doesn't relate to any known language.

The proposed algorithm can assess the proximity between two languages; in fact, when tested on known languages, it can even accurately identify language families. The team applied their algorithm to Iberian considering Basque, as well as some less-likely candidates. While Basque and Latin were closer to Iberian than other languages, they were still too different to be considered related.

In future work, the team hopes to expand their work beyond the act of connecting texts to related words in a known language—an approach referred to as "cognate-based decipherment." This paradigm assumes that such a known language exists, but the example of Iberian shows that this is not always the case. The team's new approach would involve identifying semantic meaning of the words, even if they don't know how to read them.

1. According to the author, the efforts to understand dead languages are encouraged by _____.

   A) the explorative spirit of people who spoke them

   B) the curiosity to learn a new language

   C) the pursuit for a whole body of knowledge

   D) the desire to get knowledge about the speakers

2. The word "decipher" (Line 3, Para. 2) is closest in meaning to _____.

   A) determine   B) describe   C) decode   D) declare

3. What can we learn about the new system?

   A) It has interpreted languages impossible to understand for years.

   B) It is based upon the knowledge of historic linguistics.

C) It can predict the evolution course of languages.

D) It has difficulty distinguishing related languages.

4. In Paragraph 5, the author mentions the languages of Iberian and Basque to _____.

A) exemplify the breakthrough of the new algorithm

B) illustrate the process of language development

C) overthrow the wrong concepts held for decades

D) popularize some basic knowledge of linguistics

5. The author ends his introduction to the study with _____.

A) background knowledge in its field   B) information on its future directions

C) emphasis on its significance   D) illustration of its limitations

Text 83

People rarely use just one sense to understand the world, but robots usually only rely on vision and, increasingly, touch. Carnegie Mellon University (CMU) researchers find that robot perception could improve markedly by adding another sense: hearing.

In what they say is the first large-scale study of the interactions between sound and robotic action, researchers at CMU's Robotics Institute found that sounds could help a robot differentiate between objects. Hearing also could help robots determine what type of action caused a sound and help them use sounds to predict the physical properties of new objects.

"A lot of preliminary work in other fields indicated that sound could be useful, but it wasn't clear how useful it would be in robotics," said Lerrel Pinto, who recently earned his Ph.D. in robotics at CMU and will join the faculty of New York University this fall. He and his colleagues found the performance rate was quite high, with robots that used sound successfully classifying objects 76 percent of the time. The results were so encouraging, he added, that it might prove useful to equip future robots with instrumented canes, enabling them to tap on objects they want to identify.

To perform their study, the researchers created a large dataset, simultaneously recording video and audio of 60 common objects—such as toy blocks, hand tools, shoes, apples and tennis balls—as they slid or rolled around a tray and crashed into its sides. They have since released this dataset, cataloging 15,000 interactions, for use by other researchers.

Though the size of this dataset is unprecedented, other researchers have also studied how intelligent agents can glean information from sound. For instance, Oliver Kroemer, assistant professor of robotics, led research into using sound to estimate the amount of materials, such as rice or pasta, by shaking a container, or estimating the flow of those materials from a scoop.

Pinto said the usefulness of sound for robots was therefore not surprising, though he and the others were surprised at just how useful it proved to be. They found, for instance, that a robot could use what it learned about the sound of one set of objects to make predictions about the physical properties of previously unseen objects. "I think what was really exciting was that when it failed, it would fail on things you expect it to fail on," he said. For instance, a robot couldn't use sound to tell the difference between a red block or a green block. "But if it was a different object, such as a block versus a cup, it could figure that out."

1. About the findings of this study, which of the following is true?
   A) Robots can predict actions that can cause a sound.
   B) Robots cannot use hearing to understand the world.
   C) Robots' hearing is much sharper than that of humans.
   D) Robots may use sound to distinguish different objects.

2. The researchers of the study _____.
   A) developed more advanced robots
   B) created a large dataset
   C) clarified the way to classify varied sounds
   D) identified the objects robots can recognize

3. Oliver Kroemer is cited because he _____.
   A) shared a large quantity of data
   B) found a new research direction
   C) carried out similar experiments
   D) developed some intelligent robots

4. What does Pinto mean by saying "it would fail on things you expect it to fail on"?
   A) Robots can succeed within the expected range.
   B) The hearing ability of the robots is still very limited.
   C) Robots were unable to differentiate colors of objects.
   D) The researchers expected the failure of the experiment.

5. Which of the following would be the best title for the text?
   A) To Equip Robots with "Ears"
   B) A Breakthrough in Controlling Robots
   C) The Sensory System of Robots
   D) Distinguishing Objects with Robots

(Text 84)

What if you could instruct a swarm of robots to paint a picture? The concept may sound far-fetched, but a recent study in open-access journal *Frontiers in Robotics and AI* has shown that it is possible. The robots in question move about a canvas leaving color trails in their wake, and in a first for robot-created art, an artist can select areas of the canvas to be painted a certain color and the robot team will oblige in real time. The technique illustrates the potential of robotics in creating art, and could be an interesting tool for artists.

Creating art can be labor-intensive and an epic struggle. Just ask Michelangelo about the Sistine Chapel ceiling. For a world increasingly dominated by technology and automation, creating physical art has remained a largely manual pursuit, with paint brushes and chisels still in common use. There's nothing wrong with this, but what if robotics could lend a helping hand or even expand our creative repertoire?

This latest study looks at the potential for robot swarms to create a painting. The researchers designed a system whereby an artist can designate different regions of a canvas to be painted a specific color. The robots interact with each other to achieve this, with individual robots traversing the canvas and leaving a trail of colored paint behind them, which they create by mixing paints of different colors available on-board.

In their experiments, the researchers used a projector to simulate a colored paint trail behind each robot, although they plan to develop a robot that can handle paint in the future. They found that even when some robots didn't have access to all the colors required to create the assigned color, they were still able to work together and approximate the color reasonably well.

This system could allow artists to control the robot swarm as it creates the artwork in real time. The artist doesn't need to provide instructions for each individual robot, or even worry whether they have access to all the colors needed, allowing them to focus on creating the painting.

In the current study, the resulting images are abstract, and resemble a child's crayon drawing. They show unique areas of color that flow into each other, revealing the artist's input, and are pleasing to the eye. Future versions of the system may allow for more refined images. Most importantly, the images confirm that it is possible for an artist to successfully instruct a robot swarm to paint a picture. The technique may also have potential in other fields where easily controlling the actions of a swarm of robots could be valuable. Robot orchestra, anyone?

1. The author presents a new study with _____.
   A) its background knowledge
   B) its scope of application
   C) possible doubts on it
   D) opposing views on it

2. Creating arts with robots can _____.
   A) save manpower   B) expand the scale   C) replace humans   D) spark enthusiasm

3. In this study, robots created arts by _____.
   A) choosing proper colors
   B) leaving moving trails
   C) imitating human action
   D) identifying various colors

4. In the last paragraph, the author suggests _____.
   A) the prospect of this technology
   B) the development of painting art
   C) the limitation of human ability
   D) the potential of the artists

5. Which of the following would be the best title for the text?
   A) Material Used for Making Canvas
   B) How Artists Cooperate with Robots?
   C) To Finish a Painting Without Brushes
   D) Instructing Robots to Create Paintings

(Text 85)

As part of an international collaboration, Aalto University researchers have shown that our common understanding of what attracts visual attention to screens, in fact, does not transfer to mobile applications. Despite the widespread use of mobile phones and tablets in our everyday lives, this is the first study to empirically test how users' eyes follow commonly used mobile app elements. Previous work on what attracts visual attention, or visual saliency, has centered on desktop and web-interfaces.

"Apps appear differently on a phone than on a desktop computer or browser: they're on a smaller screen which simply fits fewer elements and, instead of a horizontal view, mobile devices typically use a vertical layout. Until now it was unclear how these factors would affect how apps actually attract our eyes," explains Aalto University Professor Antti Oulasvirta.

According to previous thinking, our eyes should not only jump to bigger or brighter elements, but also stay there longer. Previous studies have also concluded that when we look at certain kinds of images, our attention is drawn to the center of screens and also spread horizontally across the screen, rather than vertically. The researchers found these principles to have little effect on mobile interfaces.

"It actually came as a surprise that bright colors didn't affect how people fixate on app details. One possible reason is that the mobile interface itself is full of glossy and colorful elements, so everything on the screen can potentially catch your attention—it's just how they're designed. It seems that when everything is made noticeable, nothing stands out in the end," says lead author and Post-doctoral Researcher Luis Leiva.

The study also confirms that some other design principles hold true for mobile apps. Gaze, for example, drifts to the top-left corner, as an indication of exploration or scanning. Text plays an important role, likely due to its role in relaying information; on first use, users thus tend to focus on text elements of a mobile app as parts of icons, labels and logos.

Image elements drew visual attention more frequently than expected for the area they cover, though the average length of time users spent looking at images was similar to other app elements. Faces, too, attracted concentrated attention, though when accompanied by text, eyes wander much closer to the location of text.

"Various factors influence where our visual attention goes. For photos, these factors include color, edges, texture and motion. But when it comes to generated visual content, such as graphical user interfaces, design composition is a critical factor to consider," says Dr. Hamed Tavakoli, who was also part of the Aalto University research team.

1. From the first paragraph, we can learn that the study _____.
    A) may get multiple countries involved   B) focuses on the development of apps
    C) uses desktops and mobile phones   D) has caused various concerns
2. According to previous thinking, _____.
    A) our eyes linger longer on brighter things   B) only certain types of images appeal to us
    C) we tend to move our eyesight vertically   D) bright colors don't affect special attention
3. The phrase "stands out" (Line 4, Para. 4) is closest in meaning to _____.
    A) proves accurate   B) gains approval   C) appears striking   D) provides basis
4. Which of the following is the finding of the new study?
    A) Bright colors shouldn't be overused.   B) Text elements have an important influence.
    C) Photos may be the most eye-catching.   D) It's unclear what affects the design of apps.
5. What is the text centered on?
    A) Traits of mobile devices.   B) Factors that attract attention.
    C) How we design mobile interfaces.   D) How mobile apps grab attention.

(Text 86)

Someday soon, an intelligent computer might create a machine far more powerful than itself. That new computer would likely make another, even more powerful, and so on. Machine intelligence would ride an exponential upward curve, attaining heights of cognition inconceivable to humans. This, broadly speaking, is the singularity.

The term dates back over 50 years, when scientists were just beginning to tinker with binary code and the circuitry that made basic computing possible. Even then, the singularity was a formidable proposition. Super intelligent computers might leap forward from nanotechnology to immersive virtual reality to superluminal space travel. Instead of being left behind with our weak, cell-based brains, humans might merge themselves with AI, augmenting our brains with circuits, or even digitally uploading our minds to outlive our bodies. The result would be a supercharged humanity, capable of thinking at the speed of light and free of biological concerns.

Philosopher Nick Bostrom thinks this could bring a new age entirely. "It might be that, in this world, we would all be more like children in a giant Disneyland—maintained not by humans, but by these machines that we have created," says Bostrom, the director of Oxford University's Future of Humanity Institute and the author of *Superintelligence: Paths, Dangers, Strategies*. Depending on where you stand, this might sound like a utopian fantasy, or a nightmare. Bostrom is well aware of this.

He's been thinking about the emergence of super intelligent AI for decades, and he's intimately familiar with the risks such creations entail. There's the classic sci-fi nightmare of a robot revolution, of course, where machines decide they'd rather be in control of the Earth. But perhaps more likely is the possibility that the moral code of a super intelligent AI—whatever that may be—simply doesn't line up with our own. An AI responsible for fleets of self-driving cars or the distribution of medical supplies could cause havoc if it fails to value human life the same way we do.

The problem of AI alignment, as it's called, has taken on new urgency in recent years, due in part to the work of futurists like Bostrom. If we cannot control a super intelligent AI, then our fate could hinge on whether future machine intelligences think like us. On that front, Bostrom reminds us that there are efforts underway to "design the AI in such a way that it would in fact choose things that are beneficial to humans, and would choose to ask us for clarification when it is uncertain what we intended."

1. Humanity may benefit from singularity by _____.
   A) replacing their cell-based brains with circuits
   B) delegating thinking to the robotic machines
   C) living spiritually longer than our physical lifespan
   D) getting rid of threats from other species

2. "Children in a giant Disneyland" is used to indicate _____.
   A) the carefree life people will live in the future
   B) the strong power of super intelligent machines

C) the illusion scientists have for human's future

D) the widespread ignorance of AI

3. Which of the following may be the risk of super intelligent AI?

A) The tension of the emergence of singularity

B) A robot revolution as described in a science fiction

C) The disorder brought about by AI failure

D) The ethical issues caused by emotionless machines

4. According to Bostrom, the researchers are working to _____.

A) address the urgency of AI alignment   B) take the advice from futurists like Bostrom

C) create robots in the interests of humans   D) provide specifications of AI performance

5. What would be the author's purpose of writing this text?

A) To warn us the might of AI.   B) To examine AI critically.

C) To compliment the insight of Bostrom.   D) To inform us of AI development.

(Text 87)

The end of the air traffic control tower is in sight after London City became the first big airport in the world to switch to a digital system. The airport has got rid of its 30-year-old tower in favour of high-definition cameras monitored by controllers sitting 70 miles away. The 16 cameras and sensors are mounted on a 50m mast, which provides a 360-degree view of the airfield.

The images, which are overlaid with other information such as aircraft speed, radar and weather readings, are designed to provide a far sharper vision of incoming and departing aircraft than is possible using human controllers alone. It will also cost less in the long term. The system has been installed in some small airports in Sweden and two years ago was introduced at Cranfield airfield in Bedfordshire. However, London City is the first large commercial airport to introduce the technology.

Air traffic control towers have been largely unchanged since the mass development of powered flight more than a century ago. It is believed that the installation of London City's digital set-up could hasten the end of control towers at other airports, which are eyeing the same technology. Heathrow—Britain's biggest airport—has previously said that it is testing the system.

Juliet Kennedy, operations director at the national air traffic service (Nats), said: "This is the UK's first major digital control tower and represents a significant technological and operational achievement. Digital tower technology tears up a blueprint that's remained largely unchanged for 100 years, allowing us to safely manage aircraft from almost anywhere, while providing our controllers with valuable new tools that would be impossible in a traditional control tower."

UK airspace is managed by air traffic controllers at several centres, including Nats's southern headquarters. Controllers direct aircraft to and from airports or ensure that they pass safely over Britain to other parts of the world.

Management of aircraft switches to staff in the control tower within a few miles of airports. This responsibility normally rests with a small dedicated team in each tower. However, under the

London City system, the remote system based on digital technology is also operated by Nats staff in Swanwick. The view of the airfield is relayed through super-fast fibre connections and displayed on 14 high-definition screens. The images can be overlaid with digital data to provide an "enhanced reality" view. Information such as call signs, altitude and speed of aircraft approaching and leaving the airport, weather readings and the ability to track moving objects can all be included in the single visual display.

1. What do we know from the first paragraph?
   A) The air traffic control tower is a landmark in London.
   B) London City airport has a history of three decades.
   C) Controllers used to work far away from the airport.
   D) The digital system allows observation from all angles.
2. It can be learned from Paragraph 2 that one benefit of the new system is _____.
   A) the improvement of aircraft speed   B) its lower cost in future
   C) its wide application in big airports   D) quick feedback from controllers
3. The example of Heathrow is used to indicate _____.
   A) the usefulness of air traffic control tower
   B) the end of outdated powered flight technique
   C) the potential for the digital system to be popularised
   D) the stability of digital control after trials
4. The author suggests in Paragraphs 4 and 5 that air traffic controllers _____.
   A) are able to perform their duties remotely   B) all work in Nats's southern headquarters
   C) only ensure the safety of British aircraft   D) are in favour of traditional control towers
5. The images from the digital tower _____.
   A) are captured by the biggest cameras   B) minimise human operations
   C) are overlaid with digital data   D) influence Nats's ability to manage airspace

(Text 88)

Take our cash, or at least our shares. That appears to be Microsoft's pet phrase these days. On April 12th the firm announced that it would acquire Nuance, a speech-recognition specialist, for nearly $20bn in cash—its second-biggest acquisition ever.

Even before this latest acquisition Microsoft had acquired a reputation for coveting tech firms that looked as alien to its core business of selling office software. "Is Satya Nadella getting bored?" wondered the Information, a website covering the tech industry. Having successfully turned Microsoft around, observers murmured, its boss might be in the grip of merger madness. In fact, there might be a method to it.

For starters, Microsoft's merger activities are unexceptional by big-tech standards, says Mark Moerdler, a broker. The industry is filled with takeover rumours; most are probably true. Large firms talk regularly to each other about potential deals. It is safe to say that Microsoft has term sheets for many potential targets on file. It still invests far more in expanding its existing businesses than on buying new ones. Excluding the Nuance deal, the company has spent only $33bn on big acquisitions in the past four years, compared with $64bn on research and development.

By its relatively timid standard, though, Microsoft has indeed become more acquisitive in recent years. Having provided textbook examples of what not to do, most notably after buying Nokia, a phonemaker, and Skype, an internet phone service, it has learned how to integrate targets successfully. Under Mr. Nadella it has taken on a shape that better lends itself to this process.

Simply put, it has become a giant computing cloud that can digest any data and offer any service. An acquisition can thus add to the business in more ways than one—and "feed the beast", in the words of Brent Thill of Jefferies, an investment bank.

Purchases also help Microsoft to keep growing rapidly by allowing it to ride big industry trends. GitHub was a bet on the shift toward creating content and related user communities, which Mr. Nadella thinks will dominate life online. Pinterest gave Microsoft access to data about people's interests, which could enable new forms of e-commerce.

The Nuance deal involves all these considerations. The firm is best known for its speech-recognition software and a health-care platform used in 77% of American hospitals. This technology, along with lots of valuable health data, will beef up Microsoft's "health cloud". Nuance's portfolio of patents can be used elsewhere in Mr. Nadella's empire. Though $20bn looks pricey for a firm with a net profit of $29m last year on revenues of $1.5bn, Microsoft can afford it. And expect Microsoft to surprise with more deals. Don't be fooled by their apparent randomness.

1. According to the first two paragraphs, Microsoft's announcement on April 12th _____.
   A) confirmed the company's transformation
   B) was regarded as a routine operation
   C) won a good reputation for its boss
   D) aroused doubts from observers
2. Microsoft's merger activities in recent years _____.
   A) were getting more ambitious
   B) cost most of its investment fund
   C) were disturbed by repeated failures
   D) became the focus of its development
3. The words of Brent Thill are cited in Paragraph 5 to show _____.
   A) the addition to Microsoft's business
   B) the trend of high-tech industry development
   C) the increasing investment of Microsoft
   D) the cruelty of commercial competition
4. The author seems to view Nadella's decision on acquisitions with _____.
   A) confusion   B) contempt   C) approval   D) surprise
5. The author discusses Microsoft's acquisition by _____.
   A) illustrating its adverse effects
   B) analyzing the causes behind it
   C) comparing varied views on it
   D) predicting its future direction

Text 89

More than 30 states are accusing Google of operating like an illegal monopoly by abusing the power it has over developers and eliminating competition in how people download and pay for apps on their Google devices. It is the latest government assault against the immense power wielded by Google amid a wave of legal and regulatory challenges rising against Big Tech in recent months.

App store commissions—typically 30%—are charged to developers, who then usually pass the cost off to consumers who are buying apps or making purchases in things like mobile games. The states' complaint zeroes in on Google's use of those fees, alleging that Google's anticompetitive policies have deprived profits from developers and raised prices on consumers.

One difference between how Apple and Google operate their devices has to do with what is known as "sideloading", the ability to download apps on a browser, instead of through an app store. Citing security concerns, Apple bans this practice, whereas Google allows it. Google additionally permits third-party app stores to be downloaded on its devices, which Apple does not permit.

However, in its lawsuit, lawyers for the states point out that Google Play's market share of apps downloaded on Google devices is more than 90%, which suggests, according to suit, that Google "faces no credible threats." Furthermore, Google prohibits competing app stores to be downloaded through its Google Play store, but rival app stores can be sideloaded onto Google devices, a process the state lawyers describe as being "unnecessarily cumbersome and impractical."

In a blog post responding to Wednesday's suit, Wilson White, Google's Senior Director of Public Policy, said the states are ignoring Google Play's openness to sideloading and third-party app stores. "This lawsuit isn't about helping the little guy or protecting consumers. It's about boosting a handful of major app developers who want the benefits of Google Play without paying for it," White wrote. "Doing so risks raising costs for small developers, impeding their ability to innovate and compete, and making apps across the Android ecosystem less secure for consumers."

The complaint from the attorneys general does not buy this, stating that: "Google's conduct has deterred new entry and prevented would-be competitors from achieving the scale that might constrain Google's power." Starting this month, Google is cutting its commission in half for the first $1 million developers make every year. It follows a similar announcement from Apple. In May, federal judge Yvonne Gonzalez Rogers told Apple CEO Tim Cook that the commission cuts do not solve larger issues about whether developers are competing on an even playing field.

1. Google has been sued in several states for _____.

   A) charging high fees from its consumers

   B) hindering competition by illegal means

   C) challenging the power of the government

   D) depriving developers of their legitimate rights

2. The phrase "zeroes in on" (Line 3, Para.2) is closest in meaning to _____.

   A) focuses on   B) objects to   C) probes into   D) discusses about

3. What do we know about "sideloading" from the text?

   A) It is complex but reasonable.   B) It affects revenue of app stores.

   C) It may bring some security risks.   D) It triggers disputes among developers.

4. A senior executive at Google holds that the states' accuses may _____.

   A) restrict Google's development ability   B) let major app developers suffer from pressure

   C) affect the apps' running environment   D) increase the burden on consumers

5. According to the federal judge, the practice of reducing commission is considered as _____.

   A) a good start to improve   B) avoidance of key problems

   C) means to mislead consumers   D) a new obstacle to competition

(Text 90)

As New York's arts groups continue to grapple with the pandemic's economic impact, the state is providing a measure of relief with its largest cultural financial commitment in recent years.

The state will provide $100 million in grants and assistance to nonprofit arts organizations during the coming year as part of the $212 billion annual budget that was approved earlier this month. That is in marked contrast to the cultural funding over the past decade, which was about $40 million a year, according to state officials. Moreover, officials pointed to other budgetary efforts to support cultural groups and businesses in both the for-profit and nonprofit realms. The goal of these efforts, said Freeman Klopott, a spokesman for the state's budget division, is to make sure cultural organizations have the resources they need to recover from the COVID-19 pandemic.

State funding generally is a small component of most nonprofit cultural groups' budgets. Even the state's $100 million commitment this year is far less than New York City's annual cultural budget, which is typically well above $150 million and has been as high as $206.9 million in recent times, according to the city's Department of Cultural Affairs.

Still, cultural groups are hailing the state's increased commitment as a welcome sign, particularly given how funding has stayed flat for so many years. Suzanne Davidson, executive director of the Chamber Music Society of Lincoln Center, another organization that is a longtime state grant recipient, said the assistance in the next year is crucial. She notes that her group is having to make financial commitments for concerts it is planning in the coming months, but it doesn't yet know how many tickets it will be allowed to sell because capacity guidance can change. The government support could go a long way to alleviate concerns, she said.

State officials said the increase in arts funding speaks to the fact that culture is increasingly being seen as an economic driver for the state, be it in arts-rich New York City or smaller upstate communities that pride themselves on their arts offerings. Mara Manus, executive director of the New York State Council on the Arts, the agency that oversees cultural funding, pointed to research that showed before the pandemic the arts sector accounted for $123 billion annually of the state's economy and provided 504,000 jobs.

Daniel O'Donnell, a Democratic state assemblyman who represents parts of Manhattan and has been a cultural advocate, said the real test will be whether the state continues to fund at this level after the pandemic. "I hope it's a first step in a long process," he said.

1. We can learn from the first two paragraphs that the new cultural funding _____.
   A) is expected to increase year by year
   B) can meet the needs of nonprofit groups
   C) will reach a total of $212 billion in a decade
   D) may help arts groups recover from the pandemic

2. According to Suzanne Davidson, arts groups _____.
   A) depend upon state budget funding   B) demand greater financial support
   C) are challenged by some uncertainties   D) are trapped by the serious fund shortage

3. Mara Manus' words are quoted to reveal _____.
   A) the increase of cultural funding
   B) the importance of the arts sector in economic development
   C) rich cultural resources of New York City
   D) contributions of the arts sector to economic recovery

4. In the last paragraph, a cultural advocate _____.
   A) expects the funding to be available quickly
   B) worries about the risks posed by the pandemic
   C) questions the possibility of subsequent support
   D) calls for continuous focus on cultural investment

5. Which of the following would be the best title for the text?
   A) New York Boosts Funding for Nonprofit Arts Groups
   B) Who Needs the Annual Cultural Budget Most?
   C) The Budget Increase of New York Arts Sector
   D) Will Government Cultural Funding Stay Flat?

(Text 91)

Cutting 20% of sugar from packaged foods and 40% from beverages could prevent 2.48 million cardiovascular disease events, 490,000 cardiovascular deaths, and 750,000 diabetes cases in the U.S. over the lifetime of the adult population, according to micro-simulation study published in *Circulation*.

A team of researchers created a model to simulate and quantify the health, economic, and equity impacts of a sugar-reduction policy proposed by the U.S. National Salt and Sugar Reduction Initiative(NSSRI). A partnership of more than 100 local, state and national health organizations convened by the New York City, Department of Health, the NSSRI released draft sugar-reduction targets for packaged foods and beverages in 15 categories in 2018. Implementing a national policy, however, will require government support to monitor companies as they work toward the targets and to publicly report on their progress. The researchers hope their model will build consensus on the need for a national-sugar reformulation policy in the US.

Ten years after the NSSRI policy goes into effect, the U.S. could expect to save $4.28 billion in total net healthcare costs, and $118.04 billion over the lifetime of the current adult population (ages 35 to 79), according to the model. Adding the societal costs of lost productivity of Americans developing diseases from excessive sugar consumption, the total cost savings of the NSSRI policy rises to $160.88 billion over the adult population's lifetime. The policy could also reduce disparities, with the greatest estimated health gains among Black and Hispanic adults, and Americans with lower income and less education—populations that consume the most sugar as a historical consequence of inequitable systems.

Product reformulation efforts have been shown to be successful in reducing other harmful nutrients. The U.S., however, lags behind other countries in implementing strong sugar-reduction policies, with countries such as the UK, Norway, and Singapore taking the lead on sugar-reformulation efforts. The US may yet become a leader in protecting its people from the dangers of excessive sugar consumption if the NSSRI's proposed sugar-reduction targets are achieved.

Consuming sugary foods and beverages is strongly linked to obesity and diseases such as type 2 diabetes and cardiovascular diseases, the leading cause of mortality in the U.S. More than two in five American adults are obese, one in two have diabetes or prediabetes, and nearly one in two have cardiovascular diseases, with those from lower-income groups being disproportionately burdened.

"Sugar is one of the most obvious additives in the food supply to reduce to reasonable amounts," says Dr. Dariush Mozaffarian. "Our findings suggest it's time to implement a national program with voluntary sugar reduction targets, which can generate major improvements in health, health disparities, and healthcare spending in less than a decade."

1. The author cites the data in the first paragraph to show that _____.

   A) it is necessary to reduce sugar intake

   B) sugar from package foods can be fatal

   C) chronic diseases are afflicting many Americans

   D) having sugar may cause various diseases

2. What can we know about NSSRI?

   A) It is a U.S. national policy issued in 2018.

   B) Many health organizations have made positive responses to it.

   C) It reports on companies' sugar-reduction progress.

   D) It is a model to simulate the sugar-reduction policy.

3. According to Paragraph 4, the U.S. _____ if the NSSRI's targets are achieved.

    A) will lag behind other countries in implementing sugar-reduction policies

    B) can be successful in reducing harmful nutrients in packaged foods

    C) is expected to become a leading country in sugar reduction

    D) is going to imitate other countries' sugar-reduction policies

4. Which of following best represents Dariush Mozaffarisn's view?

    A) Low-income people benefit the most from the NSSRI policy.

    B) It is time to control food additives at a reasonable level.

    C) It may take about a decade to realize sugar reduction targets.

    D) Social benefits of the NSSRI policy will appear in less than 10 years.

5. Which of the following can best summarize the main idea of the text?

    A) The implementation of the NSSRI policy lacks national support.

    B) A model study reveals the harm of excessive sugar intake in U.S.

    C) Reducing sugar in packaged foods can improve health greatly.

    D) Studies show the relation between chronic diseases and food additives.

(Text 92)

Britain's food supply is highly vulnerable to cyber-attacks, a leading food expert has warned, saying greater emphasis on domestic production would boost the UK's food security.

"If anyone wanted to really damage the British food system, they could just take out the satellites," said Tim Lang, professor of food policy at City, University of London. "Our 'just-in-time' system is entirely dependent on computerised logistics. When you pay for your food at the checkout, the computer isn't just adding up the bill, it's reordering the stock." An alternative report, co-authored by Lang, says the government has been complacent about food security and "places excessive reliance on others" to feed its population.

Brexit "has huge implications for food, not least since the UK's food suppliers are still closely linked with the EU's. Half a century's food links are not easily replicated by a new trade deal here or there". About a third of the food bought in the UK comes from the EU. Over the past 18 months after Brexit, the exit of EU workers from Britain has had a significant impact on food production and distribution. According to Lang, the UK should be aiming to be 80% self-sufficient in food production, compared with about 50% now. "We currently produce only 52% of the vegetables (we eat), and 10% or 11% of fruit. We import apples and pears. This is ridiculous."

Several words sum up what is needed in a new food policy, he said. "Food security—is there enough affordable, accessible, sustainable, decent food coming out of sustainable supply systems? And food defence—the need to protect supply lines."

There are enormous costs in not adopting an integrated, coherent food policy, added Lang. "Britain has turned food from being a source of life into a source of death—obesity, diabetes, strokes, lowering of life expectancy. There are also social, financial, emotional and environmental costs. We've lengthened food chains. The distance between the primary producer and the food getting into our mouths involves more and more people. The result is that in the UK we spend £225bn a year on food and drink, and the primary producers—farmers and fisherfolk—get about 7% of that."

Lang and his fellow academics have produced nine principles and tests for a comprehensive food policy that include security, resilience, food poverty and reducing the concentration of food supply in the hands of a few giant companies. Pressure must be brought to bear on the government, the report says. Lang said he hoped to sketch out a robust food policy based on sustainability. "But the issue is whether it will be taken up, or shelved, refined by the government."

1. According to the food expert, the basic way to boost Britain's food security is _____.
   A) to change the "just-in-time" system   B) to improve domestic food production
   C) the maintenance of network operation   D) the manual management of food stock
2. What brings the potential risk of cyber-attacks on British food supply?
   A) The government's overconfidence.   B) The excessive reliance on others.
   C) The computerised logistics.   D) The use of satellites.
3. It can be inferred from Paragraph 3 that Brexit has led to _____.
   A) the necessity of replicating the food links   B) failure of self-sufficient food supply
   C) manpower shortage in food industry   D) breakdown of food supply chains
4. Lang examines the current food policy mainly by _____.
   A) predicting its possible development   B) underlining its advantages
   C) analyzing its contributing factors   D) revealing its negative effects
5. How does Lang feel about the government's future food policy?
   A) Uncertain.   B) Confident.   C) Indifferent.   D) Encouraged.

Text 93

Single-use plastic plates, cutlery, and polystyrene cups will be banned in Britain under government plans, as it seeks to reduce the plastic polluting the environment.

A public consultation will launch in the autumn and the ban could be in place in a couple of years. The move was welcomed by campaigners, but they said overall progress on cutting plastic waste was "snail-paced", with the EU having banned these items and others in July. The government will also impose a plastic packaging tax from April 2022.

The government's plastic bag charge has cut their use in supermarkets by 95% since 2015, and it banned plastic microbeads in washing products in 2018. A deposit return scheme for plastic bottles will not be in place in Britain until late 2024 at the earliest, six years after being announced by the government as a key environmental policy.

The average person uses 18 throwaway plastic plates and 37 single-use knives, forks and spoons each year, while the durability of plastic litter means it kills more than a million birds and 100,000 sea mammals and turtles every year around the world. Research in 2020 found that people in the US and UK produce more plastic waste per person than any other major country. Microplastic pollution has contaminated the entire planet, from the summit of Mount Qomolangma to the deepest oceans.

Will McCallum, at Greenpeace UK, said: "Banning throwaway plastic items like plates and cutlery is a welcome move, but the UK government is simply playing catch-up with the EU. After years of talking about being a global leader in this field, the UK government has managed to crack down on a grand total of four single-use plastic items and microplastics. This snail-paced, piecemeal approach isn't leadership." McCallum said ministers should bring in legally binding targets to halve single-use plastic by 2025 and ban exports of plastic scrap. "The UK public has long been willing and ready to move on from polluting throwaway plastic," he said. "Is the government listening?"

The government intends to make companies pay the full cost of recycling and disposing of their packaging and has consulted on introducing the scheme, called "extended producer responsibility", on a phased basis from 2023. It has also consulted on plans to ensure recycling schemes are consistent across the country, with people often confused by different rules in different places. Along with businesses, the government is also taking action to tackle plastic waste through the UK Plastics Pact, which is investigating possible action by 2025 on items including crisp packets, PVC cling film, fruit and vegetable stickers, plastic coffee pods and tea bags.

1. The ban issued by the British government _____.
   A) is almost ineffective   B) is making the progress quicker
   C) will be in place in autumn   D) was welcomed by campaigners
2. Which of the following statements is true about the British government's plastic bag charge?
   A) It has banned the use of plastic items in July.
   B) It will charge plastic bottles after six years.
   C) It effectively reduced the use of plastic bags.
   D) It imposed heavy taxes on non-recycled material.
3. The data cited in Paragraph 4 put emphasis on _____.
   A) the bad effect of government policies   B) the necessity of banning plastics
   C) the popularity of plastic items   D) the solution to the plastic pollution
4. In terms of plastic ban, Will McCallum believes that Britain _____.
   A) needs to step up its action   B) becomes a popular leader
   C) must catch up with the EU   D) should restrain its ministers
5. What is this text centered on?
   A) The urgency of banning plastics.
   B) The plan to ban plastics in Britain.
   C) Social attitudes to British government policies.
   D) Environmental expectations of the public.

(Text 94)

Massachusetts is emerging as a key battleground in the U.S. fight over whether to phase out natural gas for home cooking and heating, with fears of unknown costs and unfamiliar technologies fueling much of the opposition to going all-electric. More towns around Boston are debating measures to block or limit the use of gas in new construction, citing concerns about climate change.

The measures have encountered opposition from some home builders, utilities and residents in a state with cold winters, relatively high housing prices and aging pipeline networks in need of pricey repairs.

Massachusetts debate sums up the challenges many states face in pursuing aggressive measures to reduce greenhouse-gas emissions that may directly impact consumers. The cost of fully electrifying buildings varies widely throughout the country and has ignited debates about who should potentially pay more, or change their habits, in the name of climate progress. Much resistance to electrifying new homes stems from concerns about having to heat or cook using technologies such as heat pumps and induction stoves that most have never tried.

Steve McKenna, a Massachusetts real-estate agent, was hired last year to sell a new, all-electric home in Arlington, a town that is considering gas restrictions. The home initially listed for $1.1 million, but many prospective buyers were uncomfortable with the prospect of facing higher electric bills, Mr. McKenna said. It ultimately sold for about $1 million.

Massachusetts and other states are setting goals to substantially reduce carbon emissions. Massachusetts this year passed a law requiring the state to achieve net-zero emissions by 2050. Major cities, including San Francisco, Seattle, Denver and New York, have enacted or proposed measures to ban or discourage the use of natural gas in new homes and buildings, two years after Berkeley, California passed the first such prohibition in the U.S. The efforts have sparked a backlash, prompting some states to make gas bans illegal.

The push to restrict gas use has sown concerns among home builders and real-estate agents that requiring new homes to use electricity will add to their overall cost. Construction costs for new all-electric homes are comparable with those for homes that use gas in many parts of the country, and all-electric homes can be less expensive to operate over time. But they tend to be pricier in colder climates that require more powerful heat pumps that can function in subfreezing temperatures. A study by a subsidiary of the National Association of Home Builders published this year estimated that building all-electric homes in the colder climates of Denver and Minneapolis may cost at least $11,000 more than ones that use gas.

1. The phrase "phase out" (Para. 1, Line 1) is closest in meaning to _____.
   A) decrease   B) eliminate   C) generalize   D) investigate
2. It can be learned from Paragraph 2 that many people in the U.S. _____.
   A) are reluctant to pay for the climate progress
   B) have solved the challenge of greenhouse-gas emissions
   C) prefer to use induction stoves for cooking and heating
   D) are concerned about electrification technology
3. Which of the following statements is correct about gas bans?
   A) California may be required to end its gas ban.
   B) Most of the major cities in the U.S. have issued gas bans.
   C) The measures in Massachusetts are the most radical.
   D) Gas bans had been passed in the California two years earlier than that in New York.

4. The cost of building an all-electric home _____.

   A) may differ from region to region

   B) is hard to estimate accurately

   C) will notably go down in the long run

   D) is much higher than that of building a home that uses gas

5. Which of the following would be the best title for the text?

   A) Who to Bear the Cost of Emission Reduction B) Impact of Climates on the Property Market

   C) Natural-Gas Restriction Facing Resistance   D) Efforts to Promote All-Electric Homes

(Text 95)

Ride-hailing service Uber suffered a new blow Wednesday as the European Union's top court ruled that it should be regulated like a taxi company and not a technology service, a decision that crimps its activities around Europe and could weigh on other app-based companies, too.

Uber, which is wrapping up a particularly punishing year, sought to play down the ruling Wednesday by the Luxembourg-based European Court of Justice. The company said the decision only affects its operations in four countries and it will try to keep expanding in Europe anyway. The court decision could pave the way for new regulation of other internet-based businesses, and reflects a larger dilemma about how governments should treat companies that operate online and don't fit in with traditional laws.

The decision stems from a complaint by a Barcelona taxi drivers association, which wanted to prevent Uber from setting up in the Spanish city. The taxi drivers said Uber drivers should have authorizations and licenses, and accused the company of engaging in unfair competition.

Arguing its case, San Francisco-based Uber said it should be regulated as an information services provider, because it is based on an app that connects drivers to riders. The court said in a statement that services provided by companies like Uber are "inherently linked to a transport service" and therefore must be classified as "a service in the field of transport" within EU law. It says the EU directive on electronic commerce does not apply to companies like Uber. The decision affects ride-hailing services around the 28-nation EU, where national governments can now regulate services like Uber as transport companies.

Uber said in a statement that the ruling "will not change things in most EU countries where we already operate under transportation law" and that it will "continue the dialogue with cities across Europe" to allow access to its services. The company has already been forced to adhere to national regulations in several EU countries and abandon its hallmark "peer-to-peer" service that hooks up freelance drivers and riders.

The Barcelona-based law firm representing Elite Taxi, the association that filed the lawsuit, celebrated the ruling and said it had "great judicial significance." Its consequences can be extrapolated to other businesses that keep trying to avoid legal responsibilities in the services that they provide. And the European Trade Union Confederation said in a statement that it "warmly welcomes" the judgment, saying it will help drivers get fair wages and conditions. It said the ruling "confirms that Uber does not simply exist 'on the cloud' but is well established with its wheels firmly on the road." However, an association representing online companies warned that the ruling goes against EU efforts to encourage innovation and compete with US and Asian online companies.

1. The phrase "play down" (Line 1, Para. 2) is closest in meaning to _____.
   A) pay attention to   B) struggle against
   C) reduce the effect of   D) impose pressure on
2. The dispute between Uber and the EU top court lies in their different opinions on _____.
   A) the nature of Uber's service   B) the EU directive on electronic commerce
   C) the scope of transport service   D) the application of smartphone apps
3. It is indicated in Paragraph 5 that _____.
   A) Uber's service is against the transportation law
   B) Uber's online service may be temporarily suspended
   C) Uber blocked the link between drivers and riders
   D) Uber is under the pressure of the court's ruling
4. The last paragraph displays _____.
   A) people's embrace of the court's decision   B) the self-contradiction of the court's decision
   C) possible consequences of the court's ruling   D) different attitudes toward the court's ruling
5. What is the text centered on?
   A) Uber endeavors to minimize the impact of the EU top court's ruling.
   B) The relation between Uber and the European Union has been deteriorating.
   C) Uber is to face new regulations as top EU court classifies its service as taxi service.
   D) Uber's online ride-hailing service in Europe will gradually be shrinking.

(Text 96)

The COVID-19 pandemic has prompted a group of young lawyers to launch a project to offer free legal advice remotely to anyone in the country. Dubbed the National Canadian Lawyers Initiative, the aim is to connect people in need with professionals who can offer help and direction. "The lockdown has created just a myriad of issues for people legally," said Alex Don, founder and president of the initiative. "(But) what we quickly came to understand was that this isn't just a COVID problem. This is a massive access-to-justice problem."

The project was initially slated as a "12-month sprint" in reaction to COVID-19. Among legal issues resulting from the pandemic have been those related to commercial leases, broken contracts and tenancy problems. So far, about two dozen people have made use of the service—most COVID-related—but the number was expected to grow as people learn about it.

Those accessing the service via the website need to provide contact information and indicate the legal nature of their problem. The person is then matched with an appropriate legal adviser, who, if needed, can seek help from more experienced mentors.

For now the initiative provides an opportunity for people to get urgent summary advice—more triage than an effort to take on court or other substantial legal work. Unlike traditional legal aid, people accessing the new service via the website will not have to first show they're broke. Each client, however, will be capped at a maximum of five hours of service. "We accept everyone," said Don, who was called to the bar last year. "People who can afford lawyers already have lawyers. People who really need it will come to us."

Don, who was working in Toronto before the pandemic, said he reached out to a couple of fellow McGill University-trained lawyers in early May and the initiative was federally registered late that month as a not-for-profit. The Law Society of Ontario was also quick to give its blessing, he said. The aim was to register with law societies across the country.

To date, he said, more than 300 lawyers with varying experience and law students, some of whom have lost their summer jobs due to the pandemic, have signed on to a goal of providing more than 40,000 hours of services at no charge. Most are in Ontario but others are located across the country, and their expertise spans many areas of the law. The organization has also tapped lawyers with expertise to produce answers to a list of frequently asked questions, such as on employment law or worker rights in the gig economy.

1. The word "Dubbed" (Line 2, Para. 1) is closest in meaning to _____.

   A) Known as   B) Offered to   C) Informed of   D) Organized by

2. The project initiated by Alex Don provides legal advisory services for people _____.

   A) who are troubled by the blockade   B) who cannot afford to hire a lawyer

   C) who are annoyed by trade problems   D) who like to discuss business in the bar

3. Which is the necessity for the access to this legal aid service?

   A) People need to demonstrate they are broke.

   B) People need to provide health information.

   C) People need to express their problems clearly.

   D) People need to ask for assistance within five hours.

4. The author cites the figures in the last paragraph to show _____.

   A) people are longing for more legal assistance

   B) the respect for the lawyers offering free service

   C) the project has had a wide impact

   D) the promising future of public welfare work

5. What is the text centered on?

   A) The impact of COVID-19 pandemic on legal aid.

   B) Legal problems caused by COVID-19 pandemic.

   C) Some lawyers who are dedicated to public welfare.

   D) A legal aid program amid COVID-19 pandemic.

Environmental law likely won't get the same attention as health care at next week's Senate hearings for Supreme Court nominee Amy Coney Barrett. But her confirmation, tilting the already-conservative court even further to the right, could have a major impact on the government's ability to address climate change. Nearly all of President Trump's climate rollbacks have been challenged, and several are likely headed to the high court. And some conservative allies with ties to the fossil fuel industry say they'd like to relitigate a key decision that supports climate regulations.

It's difficult to predict how Barrett would rule on specific cases. Environmental law was not her focus as a professor, and not something she dealt with a lot during her time on the U.S. Court of Appeals for the Seventh Circuit. Her judicial philosophy does offer clues. She discussed that when her nomination was announced. "A judge must apply the law, as written. Judges are not policymakers and they must be resolute in setting aside any policy views they might hold," Barrett said at a White House Rose Garden event last month.

Barrett's judicial philosophy shows skepticism of government and favors deregulation over regulation, according to Jody Freeman, who directs the Environmental and Energy Law Program at Harvard Law School and also served in the Obama administration. "I think, generally speaking, it's going to be a corporate court—good for business, good for corporations," says Freeman.

Barrett is skeptical of federal agencies stretching their authority under laws where Congress hasn't given them clear direction, but Freeman says agencies need flexibility. "Even when Congress passes new laws there are always ambiguities," Freeman says. "There always is new science, new understandings, new risks, new problems, new data. And it's impossible to specify each and every small decision that the agencies make."

As a conservative, law professor Jonathan Adler agrees that Barrett is skeptical of agencies overreaching their authority. But he says that doesn't mean Barrett is hostile to addressing climate change, just that Congress needs to pass more specific laws.

This appeals to conservatives like Tom Pyle with the American Energy Alliance, who supports Barrett's nomination and said on his podcast, "Let's duke it out where it belongs, in Congress."

But Reverend Lennox Yearwood Jr. says he wants a different kind of justice who will lead on fixing big problems like climate change. "It is a lifetime position," he says, and requires someone who "understands the nuances of the world that we live in today." He's among those who want the Senate to wait on a confirmation vote until after the presidential election.

1. According to the first paragraph, the government's ability to address climate change _____.

   A) will be discussed at the hearing next week

   B) attracts less attention than medical problems

   C) may be affected by the Supreme Court nominee

   D) is related to the development of fossil fuel industry

2. What do we know about Amy Coney Barrett?

   A) She has difficulty in dealing with specific cases.

   B) She didn't focus on environmental law.

   C) She never pays attention to environmental law.

   D) She writes laws and regulations.

3. Jody Freeman seems to view Barret's judicial philosophy with _____.

   A) discontent   B) tolerance   C) appreciation   D) respect

4. We can infer from the last paragraph that _____.

   A) Yearwood believes that climate change can be solved

   B) Yearwood suggests the amendment of environmental law

   C) Yearwood holds that judges should not focus on details

   D) Yearwood seems to disagree with Barrett's confirmation

5. What is the main message of this text?

   A) Environmental law will undergo major changes in the near future.

   B) There are quite different views on the Supreme Court nominee.

   C) The Supreme Court will reconsider climate regulations next week.

   D) The Senate should consider delaying the confirmation vote.

(Text 98)

A 1950 U.S. Supreme Court decision in a case called Feres v. United States resulted in a provision which bars active-duty military personnel from suing the government for damages. The so-called Feres Doctrine has pushed courts to throw out dozens of medical malpractice complaints.

Over the years, the Feres Doctrine has "wreaked havoc" on tens of thousands of injured military personnel and their families, says Jonathan Turley, a professor at George Washington University and an expert on the Feres Doctrine. Turley called Feres "one of the most ill considered and harmful doctrines ever created by the Supreme Court" and says the decision should be overturned entirely. It doesn't afford military members the same rights as other citizens. "There is no reason why our military should be left exposed to medical malpractice simply because they wear a uniform in defense of our country."

Nevertheless, a new law could have a profound impact on military medicine for decades to come because the military would no longer be protected from responsibility for poor outcomes of care. Claims would be handled administratively. Rather than filing a lawsuit, which might take years to rule, the Department of Defense would investigate the claim and pay using federal court guidelines.

An ongoing *U.S. News* investigation of military surgery has found that risky surgery is commonplace in military medical institutions. For instance, an analysis of five years of data from every military hospital worldwide found that surgeons in every branch of the military perform complex, high-risk operations on active-duty personnel, their family members and some retirees in such small numbers that they may put patients at risk.

U.S. News has also reported that surgical readiness is fraying fast, leaving the military unprepared to care for severe battlefield injuries. The investigation documented severe shortages of skilled surgeons, especially trauma surgeons, on active duty and in the reserves; army field hospitals that "are not staffed with appropriate specialty capabilities for a combat theater" and surgeons who operate so rarely that they can't sustain their proficiency.

Before Feres, Turley says, the military had a "reasonable approach" prohibiting military personnel from suing for wartime injuries and accidents but allowing them to sue in cases of medical negligence. Feres freed the military from responsibility for poor outcomes resulting from medical care. One extreme case, Turley says, "involved a guy who had abdominal pain. They opened him up and found a 30-inch towel that said 'Property of U.S. Army.' In any court, a jury would find negligence." Under Feres, the Supreme Court ruled, plaintiffs couldn't sue because it would affect good order and discipline.

1. From the first two paragraphs, we can infer that the Feres Doctrine _____.
   A) controlled the occurrence of medical malpractice
   B) forbade soldiers to sue in the Supreme Court
   C) deprived soldiers of the right to be equally treated
   D) has affected legal decisions on injured military members for decades
2. The word "havoc" (Line 1, Para. 2) is closest in meaning to _____.
   A) mental stress   B) legal sanction
   C) special privilege   D) damaging impact
3. The author's attitude toward the new law is one of _____.
   A) passive acceptance   B) heartfelt support
   C) slight hesitancy   D) severe criticism
4. According to *U.S. News*, military medical malpractice is mainly caused by _____.
   A) lack of medical professionals   B) negligence of the government
   C) violation of medical standards   D) poor conditions in the hospitals
5. Turley mentions one extreme case to show _____.
   A) the important role of a jury   B) shortage of military supplies
   C) irrationality of the Feres Doctrine D) universality of medical negligence

(Text 99)

Campaigners have called a law designed to reduce water pollution caused by agriculture in England "useless", as data reveals there have been no prosecutions or fines issued despite regular breaches of the rules. The Environment Agency has documented 243 violations of the "farming rules for water" since they came into effect in April 2018, according to data *The Guardian* has obtained using freedom of information legislation.

The region with the most breaches recorded was Devon and Cornwall, with 75, followed by Wessex, with 52. The recorded breaches are a fraction of the actual number, according to conservation organisations. "This legislation is being violated on a regular basis across the country by farms and virtually nothing is being done to monitor it or enforce it," said Mark Lloyd, the chief executive of the Rivers Trust, a charity that works to protect Britain's lakes and waterways. "Even when the Environment Agency identifies breaches, they don't have the resources to follow up. All of the effort put into crafting the rules and consulting on this issue has proven to be a complete waste of time."

The rules, which were announced in 2017, give the Environment Agency the power to prosecute or fine individuals and companies found to be polluting waterways with contaminated runoff water, or acting in a way that creates a high risk of pollution. Under the legislation, fixed penalties of £100 or £300 can be issued as well as "variable money penalties", which can be as much as £250,000. The rules were designed to combat agricultural pollution that is causing widespread environmental problems in rivers.

Figures released by the Environment Agency in September showed, for the first time, that no river had achieved good chemical status and only 14% of rivers were found to be of a good ecological standard. Runoff from agriculture is the biggest single polluter of rivers, responsible for 40% of damage to waterways, according to the research.

The farming rules for water focus mainly on the storage and distribution of animal waste and fertiliser to prevent damaging pollutants from farms running into rivers, where they can cause algae blooms that lead to oxygen depletion. They also require farmers to assess weather and soil conditions before spreading fertiliser to reduce the risk of it being swept into rivers and lakes. Fertiliser runoff from farmland can kill fish and plants and have a knock-on impact for other wildlife that are part of the ecosystem, such as birds.

1. According to Paragraph 1, the law regarding water pollution caused by farming is deemed futile because _____.

   A) none of the deregulations were documented

   B) statistics could not be acquired due to the information legislation

   C) the act was not in effect due to the opposition of campaigners

   D) the rule violators would not be accused or penalized

2. Mark Lloyd is quoted to indicate _____.

   A) the incapability of the Environment Agency

   B) the accurate number of breaches

   C) the achievement of the charity to protect lakes and waterways

   D) the effort to craft the rules and consult on this issue

3. One motive in crafting the rules is to _____.

   A) protect lakes and rivers from being contaminated by farming practice

   B) prosecute countries that pollute waterways

   C) regulate agricultural activities

   D) preserve wildlife in lakes and waterways

4. It is argued that fertiliser runoff from farmlands to rivers and lakes could be _____.

    A) assessed   B) prevented   C) disastrous   D) reduced

5. Which of the following would be the best title for the text?

    A) Failure to Protect Rivers   B) Invalid Law Enforcement

    C) Dangers of Farm Pollutants   D) The Enactment of a Law

(Text 100)

Letitia James, New York's attorney-general, couldn't be blunter in describing the antitrust case lodged on December 9th against the world's biggest social network. "By using its vast amounts of data and money Facebook has squashed or hindered what the company perceived as potential threats. They've reduced choices for consumers, they suppressed innovation and they degraded privacy protections for millions of Americans," she declared, summarising the accusations. Forty-five states joined her bipartisan coalition against the giant. Separately, the Federal Trade Commission (FTC) sued Facebook for monopolistic practices in social-networking and demanded remedies including the firm's break-up.

A few years ago co-ordinated action by 46 states and the FTC that could split Facebook apart was unthinkable, says Lina Khan, an antitrust scholar at Columbia Law School. But the case is about more than narrow competition law. The controversies around Facebook's privacy practices, the spread of fake news and conspiracy theories on the platform, and its exploitation by authoritarian regimes mean regulators and politicians are set on forcing change.

Will they succeed? The cases look strong. Experts judge Facebook to be the lowest-hanging antitrust fruit, alongside Google (which America's Justice Department sued over alleged monopoly abuses in October). Amazon and Apple may become the targets, but those cases will take longer, if they come at all, says an antitrust expert.

The Facebook lawsuits centre on its acquisitions. The firm maintained its monopoly in personal social-networking by systematically buying up potential competitors, both contend—notably Instagram in 2012 and WhatsApp in 2014. Another alleged anti-competitive practice was blocking rival app developers from its platform. As consumer harm is hard to prove against big tech's mostly free products, the suits try a novel argument: that damage is done to users' privacy and advertisers' choice.

Facebook will argue that its market is social media, which is broader and more competitive than social-networking. Tik Tok, a Chinese-owned short-video app, is now more popular than Instagram among American teenagers. The internal Facebook emails on which the lawsuits hinge hardly paint a picture of a lazy monopolist; Mr. Zuckerberg and his lieutenants see competitive threats everywhere. Facebook can also argue that breaking it up is almost impossible. Last year it started integrating Instagram, WhatsApp and Messenger more deeply. And the FTC's complaint fails to mention it cleared the Instagram and WhatsApp deals. The government "now wants a do-over", sending a chilling warning to American business that "no sale will ever be final", Facebook said.

Markets shrugged off the news. Facebook's shares dipped by 2%, in line with the rest of big tech. Investors either see forced break-up as unlikely, says Brent Thill of Jefferies, an investment bank—or spy even more money to be made from it.

1. According to Letitia James, Facebook should be accused of _____.
   A) neglecting its product innovation   B) using a large data pool improperly
   C) depriving users of the right to choose D) stealing customers' private information
2. It can be inferred from Paragraph 3 that _____.
   A) Facebook could be split up   B) Google will fail in the antitrust lawsuit
   C) Apple and Amazon will be prosecuted   D) other tech giants may face antitrust problems
3. According to the prosecution, Facebook's practice _____.
   A) hinders the development of social platforms B) cuts off competitors from advertisers
   C) damages the privacy of consumers   D) stops the free use of the rival apps
4. Facebook defends itself by arguing that _____.
   A) it is not as competitive as other social networks
   B) its acquisitions are officially approved
   C) it is threatened by the U.S. government
   D) the evidence against it is not entirely true
5. Investors' attitude towards the antitrust case is _____.
   A) indifferent   B) sarcastic   C) doubtful   D) critical

答案速查

第 1 章

Text 1	1. B	2. C	3. D	4. A	5. D	Text 10	1. D	2. A	3. D	4. B	5. C
Text 2	1. A	2. D	3. C	4. B	5. C	Text 11	1. C	2. D	3. A	4. B	5. D
Text 3	1. A	2. D	3. D	4. B	5. C	Text 12	1. A	2. C	3. A	4. D	5. D
Text 4	1. B	2. C	3. A	4. B	5. D	Text 13	1. B	2. A	3. C	4. C	5. A
Text 5	1. B	2. C	3. D	4. C	5. A	Text 14	1. C	2. D	3. B	4. A	5. D
Text 6	1. C	2. A	3. D	4. D	5. B	Text 15	1. C	2. D	3. B	4. A	5. A
Text 7	1. A	2. C	3. B	4. C	5. D	Text 16	1. D	2. B	3. C	4. C	5. C
Text 8	1. B	2. A	3. B	4. D	5. C	Text 17	1. C	2. B	3. D	4. A	5. C
Text 9	1. C	2. A	3. D	4. B	5. B						

第 2 章

Text 18	1. D	2. A	3. C	4. B	5. A	Text 27	1. C	2. B	3. D	4. D	5. A
Text 19	1. B	2. D	3. B	4. C	5. A	Text 28	1. B	2. A	3. C	4. B	5. D
Text 20	1. A	2. C	3. B	4. C	5. A	Text 29	1. D	2. C	3. D	4. B	5. A
Text 21	1. A	2. B	3. B	4. C	5. D	Text 30	1. D	2. A	3. C	4. B	5. B
Text 22	1. A	2. C	3. B	4. D	5. C	Text 31	1. C	2. A	3. A	4. C	5. B
Text 23	1. C	2. A	3. B	4. D	5. C	Text 32	1. B	2. A	3. D	4. D	5. C
Text 24	1. A	2. D	3. C	4. D	5. C	Text 33	1. C	2. A	3. D	4. C	5. B
Text 25	1. A	2. C	3. B	4. B	5. D	Text 34	1. D	2. A	3. C	4. B	5. A
Text 26	1. A	2. B	3. C	4. D	5. D						

第 3 章

Text 35	1. C	2. A	3. C	4. B	5. D	Text 43	1. D	2. D	3. C	4. A	5. B
Text 36	1. D	2. C	3. C	4. A	5. B	Text 44	1. B	2. C	3. D	4. A	5. B
Text 37	1. C	2. B	3. B	4. D	5. A	Text 45	1. C	2. C	3. B	4. A	5. D
Text 38	1. D	2. A	3. B	4. C	5. C	Text 46	1. C	2. A	3. B	4. A	5. D
Text 39	1. B	2. C	3. A	4. D	5. A	Text 47	1. B	2. D	3. B	4. C	5. A
Text 40	1. A	2. D	3. B	4. C	5. C	Text 48	1. D	2. A	3. B	4. B	5. C
Text 41	1. A	2. C	3. B	4. C	5. A	Text 49	1. B	2. C	3. D	4. A	5. A
Text 42	1. C	2. A	3. C	4. D	5. B						

第 4 章

Text 50	1. C	2. D	3. B	4. A	5. C	Text 52	1. A	2. B	3. D	4. C	5. A
Text 51	1. A	2. D	3. B	4. A	5. C	Text 53	1. B	2. D	3. A	4. C	5. B

Text 54	1. B	2. C	3. C	4. A	5. D	Text 59	1. A	2. B	3. D	4. C	5. D
Text 55	1. B	2. C	3. A	4. D	5. A	Text 60	1. C	2. A	3. A	4. D	5. B
Text 56	1. D	2. A	3. C	4. C	5. B	Text 61	1. D	2. C	3. C	4. A	5. B
Text 57	1. D	2. A	3. A	4. C	5. B	Text 62	1. A	2. B	3. A	4. C	5. D
Text 58	1. A	2. A	3. C	4. D	5. B	Text 63	1. B	2. C	3. D	4. C	5. A

第 5 章

Text 64	1. D	2. C	3. A	4. A	5. B	Text 71	1. B	2. A	3. D	4. C	5. B
Text 65	1. B	2. D	3. C	4. A	5. D	Text 72	1. C	2. B	3. B	4. A	5. B
Text 66	1. C	2. A	3. A	4. B	5. D	Text 73	1. D	2. B	3. D	4. C	5. A
Text 67	1. A	2. C	3. A	4. B	5. D	Text 74	1. A	2. C	3. D	4. B	5. B
Text 68	1. C	2. B	3. B	4. A	5. D	Text 75	1. B	2. D	3. C	4. A	5. B
Text 69	1. D	2. A	3. D	4. D	5. B	Text 76	1. A	2. C	3. A	4. D	5. B
Text 70	1. A	2. D	3. C	4. A	5. B

第 6 章

Text 77	1. C	2. D	3. A	4. B	5. B	Text 83	1. D	2. B	3. C	4. A	5. A
Text 78	1. A	2. B	3. C	4. B	5. D	Text 84	1. C	2. A	3. B	4. A	5. D
Text 79	1. D	2. A	3. B	4. B	5. C	Text 85	1. A	2. A	3. C	4. B	5. D
Text 80	1. B	2. B	3. D	4. A	5. C	Text 86	1. C	2. B	3. D	4. C	5. B
Text 81	1. B	2. A	3. C	4. A	5. C	Text 87	1. D	2. B	3. C	4. A	5. C
Text 82	1. D	2. C	3. B	4. A	5. B	Text 88	1. D	2. A	3. A	4. C	5. B

第 7 章

Text 89	1. B	2. A	3. C	4. C	5. B	Text 95	1. C	2. A	3. D	4. D	5. C
Text 90	1. D	2. C	3. B	4. D	5. A	Text 96	1. A	2. B	3. C	4. C	5. D
Text 91	1. A	2. B	3. C	4. D	5. C	Text 97	1. C	2. B	3. A	4. D	5. B
Text 92	1. B	2. C	3. C	4. D	5. A	Text 98	1. D	2. D	3. B	4. A	5. C
Text 93	1. D	2. C	3. B	4. A	5. B	Text 99	1. D	2. A	3. A	4. C	5. B
Text 94	1. B	2. D	3. D	4. A	5. C	Text 100	1. B	2. D	3. C	4. B	5. A